bread machine
easy

bread machine
easy

70 delicious recipes that make
the most of your machine

Sara Lewis

hamlyn

An Hachette UK Company
www.hachette.co.uk

First published in Great Britain in 2008 by Hamlyn,
a division of Octopus Publishing Group Ltd,
Endeavour House, 189 Shaftesbury Avenue
London WC2H 8JY
www.octopusbooks.co.uk
www.octopusbooksusa.com

First published in paperback in 2010

Copyright © Octopus Publishing Group Ltd 2008

Distributed in the U.S. and Canada by Octopus Books USA:
c/o Hachette Book Group
237 Park Avenue, New York NY 10017

ISBN 978-0-600-62182-9

A CIP catalogue record for this book is available from the British
Library

Printed and bound in China
10 9 8 7 6 5 4 3 2 1

Notes

Standard level spoon measures are used in all recipes
1 tablespoon = one 15 ml spoon
1 teaspoon = one 5 ml spoon

Both metric and imperial measurements are given for the recipes. Use
one set of measures only, not a mixture of both. All recipes have been
tested in metric.

This book includes dishes made with nuts and nut derivatives. It is
advisable for those with known allergic reactions to nuts and nut
derivatives and those who may be potentially vulnerable to these
allergies, such as pregnant and nursing mothers, invalids, the elderly,
babies and children, to avoid dishes made with nuts and nut oils. It is
also prudent to check the labels of pre-prepared ingredients for the
possible inclusion of nut derivatives.

Medium eggs have been used throughout.
Fresh herbs were used unless otherwise stated.

A range of bread-making machines were used to test these recipes.
Because machines vary considerably in size and in the length and type
of programme, refer to the manufacturer's handbook and adjust the
ingredient amounts and the order in which they are added or change
to a different programme if the handbook suggests otherwise.

Notes for American readers
Ingredients: equivalents and substitutions

UK	US
almond essence	almond extract
beetroot	beet
bicarbonate of soda	baking soda
black treacle	molasses
bun	roll
caster sugar	superfine sugar
celery sticks	celery stalks
chilli	chile
clotted cream	Devonshire cream
cocoa	cocoa powder
crème fraîche	sour cream
desiccated coconut	shredded coconut
fast-action dried yeast	quick-rising active dry yeast
flaked almonds	slivered almonds
glacé cherries	candied cherries
glacé ginger	crystallized ginger
golden syrup	light corn syrup
Greek yogurt	whole milk yogurt
Guinness	stout
icing sugar	confectioners' sugar
jam	jelly
linseeds	flaxseeds
muscovado sugar	brown sugar
natural yogurt	plain yogurt
orange marmalade	citrus jelly
pepper, red/green/yellow	bell pepper
plain dark chocolate	bittersweet chocolate
plain flour	all-purpose flour
rocket	arugula
self-raising flour	self-rising flour
spring onion	scallion
stoned dates	pitted dates
stoned prunes	pitted prunes
strong flour	bread flour
strong granary flour	strong whole grain flour
strong malthouse flour	strong malted grain flour
strong wholemeal flour	strong whole wheat flour
sugar lumps	sugar cubes
sultana	golden raisin
wholemeal flour	whole wheat flour

Approximate conversions

60 ml (2 fl oz)	¼ US cup
120 ml (4 fl oz)	½ US cup
180 ml (6 fl oz)	¾ US cup
240 ml (8 fl oz)	1 US cup
1 litre (1¾ UK pints)	4 US cups

Some standard equivalents

The following are the
   equivalent of 1 US cup:
125 g (4 oz) flour
225 g (8 oz) granulated or
   caster (superfine) sugar
125 g (4 oz) icing
   (confectioners') sugar
225 g (8 oz) butter
200 g (6 oz) rice

Contents

Introduction

All those frustrated, overworked wanna-be cooks can now unleash the domestic goddess within and fill their homes with the wonderful aroma of freshly baked bread. Using a bread machine may make you feel as if you're cheating, but who really has time to make bread by hand these days? Simply weigh the ingredients, add them to the machine and walk away. What could be easier? And it really is a great way to impress family and friends.

With 70 recipes to choose from, there is something here for every occasion, from easy everyday classics for breakfast toast and sandwiches for packed lunches to smarter gourmet breads that you can share with friends over an informal lunch of salad or soup or as an accompaniment to a slow-cooked casserole. You will also find some delicious wheat-free recipes too.

Give the children an after-school treat that isn't packed with additives and preservatives by serving a warm slice of a sweet and fruity bread, or for those moments when you do have a bit more time set the bread machine to dough only and shape the breads yourself into rustic-looking, garlicky olive foccacia or stuffed schiacciatas, or professional-looking gingered banana spirals or a splendid cherry and frangipane twist. Lure the kids away from the TV on a wet afternoon and make homemade pizzas, mini iced buns or easy iced rabbits.

Leave the bread machine on the work surface so that it is always ready

for action. And don't forget that you can set the delay timer before you go to bed and then wake up to the delicious aroma of freshly baked bread, enjoyed with a mug of hot chocolate or strong coffee – a perfect and relaxing way to begin the weekend or to get a midweek morning off to a good start.

What ingredients do I need?

The ingredients for machine-made bread are the same as for hand-made bread. Always read the machine manufacturer's handbook for precise quantities.

Yeast

The most important ingredient of all, yeast is activated by water and fed by sugar, and as it ferments it makes tiny bubbles of carbon dioxide gas that cause the dough to rise. As the bread rises, it is supported by gluten, an elastic protein found in wheat flours, which allows the dough to stretch and hold in the gas bubbles.

Although yeast is available in three forms – fresh, dried (which must be activated in warm water before use) and fast-action dried yeast – the last of these, fast-action dried yeast, is best suited to making bread in a bread machine. Buy it in small sachets or packs and make sure that you measure it accurately with level spoon measures. A rounded teaspoon may give almost an extra level ¼ teaspoon yeast or the difference between a nicely domed loaf and one that sticks to the lid of your bread machine.

Add the yeast to the bread machine last and keep it in a little nest of flour and sugar. This is especially important if you are going to use the delay timer programme, because once the yeast gets wet it will begin to ferment, and if this happen before the kneader blade is activated the yeast will have run out of steam before the bread is mixed.

Wheat flours

Most supermarkets now sell a wide range of flours for bread making, but for well-risen bread it is important to choose a flour that has been milled from a hard wheat with a high gluten content, usually labelled 'strong' or 'bread' flour. Alternatively, mix flours with a low gluten content, such as rye, with a flour that contains more gluten.

As a guide, the more gluten there is, the higher the bread will rise. Semolina flour is milled from the endosperm of durum wheat, so it is high in gluten. It is traditionally made into pasta, but it can also be used for bread making but must be mixed with white bread flour, or the bread will be heavy. Plain white flours may be used in teabreads, and they are usually mixed with baking powder or bicarbonate of soda rather than yeast.

Wholewheat or wholemeal flours contain bran and wheatgerm as well as the endosperm, and once again you should choose 'strong' or 'bread' flour. Because bran inhibits the release of gluten, these flours rise more slowly, hence the longer programme times in the machine. Mix them with powdered vitamin C to boost the rise or mix wholewheat flour with white bread flour for a lighter loaf. Malthouse flour, which is made with a mix of wholewheat and rye flours with added malted wheat grains, or granary flour, a mix of wholemeal, white and rye flours with added malted wheat flakes, will produce a lighter option.

Spelt flour, which has been milled since Roman times, is a high-protein wheat flour, but it has less gluten than other wheat flours so will produce a closer textured bread. It is best baked in machines with programmes between 2 hours 50 minutes and 4 hours only: any longer and the bread may collapse. Because there is less gluten it may be tolerated by those who find wheat products difficult to digest. It is available as a nutty-tasting wholemeal or lighter white bread flour.

Non-wheat flours

Buckwheat is something of a misnomer, because the flour is milled from a seed related to the rhubarb family and does not contain wheat at all. It is greyish-brown in colour and has a strong, earthy flavour. Because it is low in gluten it should be mixed with other flours to help it rise.

Rye, which is also low in gluten, is a strong-tasting, dark-coloured flour that must be mixed with other flours for best results. It is most commonly used in Scandinavian and Russian black breads.

Millet flour, a pale yellow flour that is high in protein, is low in gluten. It has a slightly gritty texture, and it may give a crumbly texture to finished breads.

Barley flour is a mild flour with a sweet, earthy taste. Use it in small quantities in bread, or it will produce a bread with a close, cake-like texture.

Gluten-free flours

People who have to follow a gluten-free diet often find that giving up traditional bread is one of the hardest things to do. It has always been difficult to replicate the characteristics of gluten, but now many large supermarkets and health food stores are selling blends of gluten-free flours with added natural gum. Made with a mix of rice, potato and tapioca flours with the addition of xanthum gum, this makes a much more convenient and hassle-free way of making your own bread at a fraction of the cost of specialist bought breads.

If you would rather make up your own flour blends choose from gram or chickpea flour, ground cornmeal or masa harina (which should not be confused with white cornflour), quinoa flour (which is ground from a nutty-tasting grain from Peru and is rich in protein) or soya bean flour (which is high in protein but has a slightly bitter taste). Mix your chosen flour with powdered xanthum gum, which is available from some large supermarkets, by mail order or via the internet.

Sugar

Sugar is essential to feed the yeast. Just 1 teaspoon per 500 g (1 lb) flour is all that is required, but you may add more to flavour the bread. If you add too much sugar the yeast will be inhibited. Choose from white, light or dark muscovado, or try adding honey, maple syrup or malted yeast extract. Sugar scorches easily, so for sweet breads, where the amounts used are higher, make sure that you use the sweet programme, with its lower baking temperature, so that the crust is not over-browned. Do not use artificial sweeteners.

Enriching ingredients

Butter, oil and eggs all add richness to the finished bread, so, too, do yogurt, soured cream (or crème fraîche), cream cheese or harder cheeses, producing a softer, more tender crumb. Butter and oil also act as preservatives and keep bread fresher for longer. Make sure the butter is at room temperature so that it is easy to scoop into a tablespoon; make sure that the spoon is level.

Do not use the delay timer programme if you are adding fresh dairy products or eggs. Breads such as French bread, which are made without butter or oil, must be eaten on the day they are made.

Salt

Not only is salt needed to enhance the flavour of the bread, but it is also required to control the rate at which the yeast ferments, which, in turn, strengthens the gluten and stops the bread from rising too much and then collapsing. Salt and yeast should be added to the bread machine so that they do not come into contact with each other before the dough is mixed. As with sugar, if too much salt is added the yeast will be inhibited. Do not use salt substitutes.

Water

Unlike when you are making bread by hand, most recipes for machine-made bread require the addition of cold water, but do check with the manufacturer's handbook before you use your machine for the first time. The only exceptions are when you are baking on the fastbake or rapid programme, when the time is so short. The water should feel just warm to your little finger – if it is too hot the yeast will be killed; if it is too cold the yeast won't be activated in time.

Special diets

If you are using a bread machine for wheat- and gluten-free cooking, it is vital that you take extra care when washing out the tin and kneader blade. Even the slightest trace of wheat products in the machine might cause an allergic reaction in someone who suffers with coeliac disease.

Choosing the right programme

Basic white bread

You will probably use this setting more than any other, and it can be used for plain white bread, flavoured breads or enriched breads. This is an ideal programme for using the delay timer.

Wholewheat

Because wholewheat bread tends to be heavier, this programme is longer and has a greater preheat time to allow the grain to soak up the water and expand. Depending on your machine, the time may vary between 3½ and 5 hours, and for those machines with a long programme the bread may have three risings for a lighter crumb.

Rapid or fastbake

This ultra-quick programme takes around 1 hour, and unlike most bread machine recipes the water must be warm when it is added to activate the yeast quickly. Because rising times are so short, extra yeast is required so that the finished bread is light and well risen.

Sweet

Sweeter breads tend to brown more quickly than ordinary ones, so this programme makes sure that they have sufficient time to rise and a lower temperature to bake in.

Cakes

This short programme takes from 1 hour 40 to 1 hour 50 minutes, depending on the machine, and it is ideal for yeast-free teabreads or small cakes. Unlike the bread recipes, the cakes will be smaller, about 8 cm (3 inches) high, after baking. Baking powder or bicarbonate of soda mixed with plain flour or self-raising flour is used in place of yeast, and because there is no yeast the mixture is not left to rise. Check the cakes after 1 hour 40 minutes by inserting a skewer into the centre. If it comes out sticky leave the cake in for 10 minutes more and then retest or leave the cake to finish cooking with the keep-warm facility.

Dough

The dough is mixed, kneaded and left to rise twice. Scoop the dough out of the bread pan and then knead by hand, adding extra flavourings if you like. Shape the dough, then leave it to rise in a warm place loosely covered with oiled clingfilm and bake in the conventional way.

Additional programmes

French This programme has a longer rising time, so it produces a bread with a lighter, more open texture. Some machines also cook the bread at a higher temperature for a crisper crust. Use for low-fat, low-sugar breads only.

Sandwich This is designed to produce a light-textured loaf with a softer but thicker crust.

Speciality Breads baked on this slightly shorter programme tend to have a closer texture.

Extra bake This facility enables you to use the bread machine as an oven only, so it is ideal for baking a small cake or teabread. Unlike the other programmes, the ingredients must be mixed together before being added to the bread pan. Alternatively, the programme can be used to lengthen the cooking time once a selected programme has finished.

Keep-warm facility Once the bread is baked, the keep-warm facility will circulate hot air for a further 30–60 minutes, depending on the machine and size of loaf. For best results remove the loaf within this time, because after that the steam from the bread will condense and may make it go soggy. A series of beeps will remind you to remove the bread.

Delay timer This is a great option, enabling you to put all the ingredients into the bread machine before you go to bed or off to work so that the bread is ready at a time that suits you. Do not add perishable ingredients, such as fresh milk and eggs.

Jam The bread pan can also be used to make small quantities of jam and marmalade. See the manufacturer's handbook for instructions.

Step by step to the perfect loaf

1 Before you begin Stand the bread machine, unplugged, on the work surface and make sure there is plenty of space for air to circulate around it. Fit the kneader blade in the bread pan. If the blade folds down at the end of cooking, make sure that it is vertical at this stage.

2 Adding liquid Add warm or cold water or milk as the handbook advises. Add dried milk powder if you are using the delay timer programme.

3 Enriching the mixture To add richness and so that the bread keeps fresher for longer, add sunflower or olive oil. If you prefer to use butter, make sure that it is soft and at room temperature for easy mixing. For larger amounts of butter, melt it first. Add beaten eggs at this stage if required.

4 Adding dry ingredients Spoon in salt and any spices or powdered flavourings at this point, then spoon the flour or a mix of strong bread flours on top of the liquid to cover it completely. Make a slight dip in the centre.

5 **Adding raising agents** Using level teaspoon measures, add the sugar and fast-action dried yeast to the dip in the flour. Make sure that neither the sugar nor the yeast comes into contact with the water at this point. This is especially important if you are using the delay timer setting because the yeast will begin to ferment before the machine has started. Select the size of loaf, programme and crust colour you want, then press start.

6 **Adding additional ingredients after kneading** A beeper will sound during the second dough kneading. Gradually add additional ingredients, such as sun-dried tomatoes, chopped spring onions, muesli, nuts or dried fruit, so that the kneader blade does not become clogged up.

7 **Dough after rising** At the end of the final rising the bread dough may be glazed with milk or a mixture of egg yolk and water, then sprinkled with seeds, oats or nuts and left to bake. Open and close the lid carefully and try to keep the lid open for the shortest time possible so that the cold air does not make the bread sink.

Check the handbook

Not all bread machines are the same, so always look at the handbook or manual that came with your machine before you try a recipe for the first time. Alter the amounts of yeast or other ingredients according to the manufacturer's directions if necessary. You may also need to add the ingredients in the order that the manufacturer specifies if this differs from the steps shown in this book.

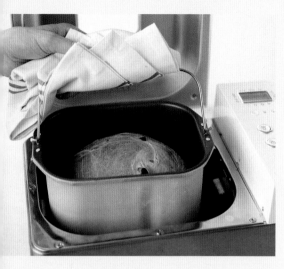

8 **Baked bread** At the end of the programme, the machine will beep to tell you that it has finished. Open the lid and, using oven gloves or a tea towel, lift the bread pan out of the machine, twisting it if required and using the handle if there is one.

9 **Loosening the bread with a plastic spatula** Loosen the edges of the bread with a plastic spatula so that you do not scratch the nonstick pan, then turn the bread out on to a wire rack, removing the kneader blade from the base if necessary. Sprinkle the bread with a little flour if it is not already glazed.

Size matters
Bread machines vary in size, with bread pans that range in capacity from 1.3 litres (2¼ pints) up to 3.3 litres (5¾ pints) or that can make a 500 g (1 lb) loaf up to a 1 kg (2 lb) one. Most machines are designed to make two different sizes of loaf and will have a different setting for each size to alter the cooking times. The recipes in this book have been developed to make a 750 g (1½ lb) loaf and will fit in a bread pan with a capacity of 2.5 litres (4 pints) and above. The accurate measurement of all ingredients with a measuring jug, measuring spoons and scales is vital. Keep to either metric or imperial measurements; do not interchange between the two.

Upper crust
Some machines have three crust settings for light, medium and dark. Choose your family's favourite, but remember that in general the more fat and sugar there are, the darker the bread will be. For richer mixtures, therefore, select the light crust option so that the finished bread will have a gold-coloured crust.

Making the most of your bread machine

Finishes

Although you will most often put the ingredients for your selected recipe in the machine and then go away and forget about it until the beeper reminds you that it is ready, there will be times — perhaps when you have friends coming for lunch — when you would like to do something extra special. Adding a glaze or finish to your bread will take just a few minutes but will add that professional touch.

Before baking

Check with your machine's handbook and work out when cooking will commence, then brush the top of the bread about 10 minutes before baking begins with one of the following finishes. Open and shut the lid of the bread machine gently and try to keep the lid open for as short a time as possible so that the temperature does not drop too much.

Egg yolk and water Mix 1 egg yolk with 1 tablespoon cold water and brush it over risen dough for a shiny golden glaze. Egg yolk is better than a whole beaten egg, which tends to go streaky.

Egg white and water Use 1 egg white mixed with 1 tablespoon cold water for a paler crust with a soft sheen.

Milk Brush this over risen dough for a soft crust and as 'glue' for sticking grains and seeds to the top of breads.

Salted water Mix 3 teaspoons salt with 3 tablespoons water and brush over risen dough to produce a crisp crust. To make a less salty version, add 1 teaspoon caster sugar.

Olive oil Drizzle the oil over Italian-style breads before and after baking for a soft, glistening finish. Choose virgin olive oil for a stronger flavour.

After baking

Finish your loaf after baking with one of these sweet or savoury suggestions.

Flour Sprinkle the baked loaf with a little flour and then leave to cool.

Butter Rub a small knob of butter over the top of a pale baked loaf and then brown under a hot grill.

Preserves Warm 2 tablespoons marmalade or apricot jam with 2 teaspoons water in a small saucepan, then brush over the top of a baked bread or teabread for a glossy but sticky finish.

Milk and sugar glaze Dissolve 1 tablespoon caster sugar in 2 tablespoons milk in a small pan. Brush over sweet breads the moment they come out of the oven for an extremely glossy finish.

Honey or golden syrup Warm a little honey or syrup in a saucepan or the microwave and brush over sweet breads the moment they come out of the oven for a glossy but sticky glaze.

Glacé icing Mix 125 g (4 oz) sifted icing sugar with 4–5 teaspoons water, lemon or orange juice to make a smooth, spoonable icing. Drizzle it over cooled baked breads.

Dusting of sugar Sift a little sifted icing sugar over the top of a sweet bread for a quick and attractive finish.

Additional finishes

If you are brushing a bread with an egg yolk or plain milk glaze you might also like to scatter the top with one of the ingredients that is already included in it as a visual clue to the flavour of the bread: sprinkle with rye flakes for a bread made with a mix of rye and wholemeal flour, muesli for a muesli loaf and so on. Poppy, pumpkin, sunflower and linseeds look attractive, as do a few roughly chopped nuts, ground spices, coarse sea salt or grated cheese.

For sweet breads add some roughly crushed sugar lumps, diced chocolate or flaked almonds.

Adapting recipes to make different sized breads

If you want to make larger or smaller loaves or adapt a favourite recipe not originally meant for a bread machine, base the ingredients and method on one of the recipes in this book that you have made and know fits your machine. Alternatively, find a similar recipe in the manufacturer's handbook. Add up the total weight of the dry ingredients so that the flour and flavourings, such as muesli, seeds, nuts or dried fruit, do not exceed the amount originally indicated. Then work back, keeping the proportions as close to the tested recipe as possible.

Storing bread

Homemade bread is best eaten on the day that it is made, but it can be kept fresh for a day or two if oil or butter has been added. Unlike shop-bought bread, there are no preservatives or additives to lengthen shelf life. For a family this is not usually a problem because the bread will quickly disappear before the day is over.

If there are just two of you, halve the bread and freeze half for another day. If you prefer, slice the bread and freeze slices in resealable plastic bags. Take out as many as you need, when you need them and make them into sandwiches while still frozen. Place on a sheet of kitchen paper inside a plastic bag or foil so that the sandwiches will not go soggy as the bread thaws.

Using leftovers

Make any slightly stale bread into toast, bruschetta or one of the ideas below.

French toast

Fork 2 eggs with 2 tablespoons milk in a shallow dish, add halved slices of bread and dip both sides into the egg until well coated. Fry in a little melted butter and oil until crisp and golden, then serve sprinkled with a little caster sugar and some ground cinnamon. Top with spoonfuls of Greek yogurt and a few sliced strawberries and some blueberries if you have them.

Bread and butter pudding

This needn't be made with plain white bread — it's delicious made with flavoured sweet breads or with sweetened oaty or mixed-grain breads, thinly sliced and buttered, then layered in an ovenproof dish with dried fruits and baked with a vanilla egg custard.

For a Paddington pudding, spread the buttered bread with a little marmalade; for a chocolate bread-and-butter pudding layer buttered bread with a little melted chocolate mixed with a knob of butter.

Breadcrumbs

Make smaller amounts of leftover bread into crumbs in a liquidizer or food processor, then spoon into a plastic box and freeze. There's no need to defrost first — simply take out a spoonful or two and sprinkle over gratin-style dishes. You can mix the breadcrumbs with chopped olives, basil, sun-dried tomatoes, lemon rind and juice and a little olive oil as a topping for salmon or cod steaks or mackerel fillets. Bake until golden and serve with salad for an easy midweek supper. The breadcrumbs can also be used to make stuffings to go with a Sunday roast.

Troubleshooting

Why do the ingredients have to be added in a particular order?

In general, the wet ingredients are put into the bread machine first because this allows the kneader blade to work most efficiently, gradually mixing in the flour, then, last of all, the sugar and yeast once the heating element has begun to warm the machine. This is especially important if you are using the delay timer programme because the yeast needs to be kept dry while it waits.

The bread did not rise. Why?

You didn't use enough yeast. Did you use ordinary kitchen teaspoons so the amount was not accurately measured?

It could have been that the yeast was out of date.

Did you use the right kind of dried yeast? All the recipes in this book use fast-action dried yeast, which does not need to be left to froth in warm water before use but can be mixed straight into dry ingredients. Double-check with the directions on the yeast packet.

The plug was accidentally turned off while a programme was under way. What can I do?

Don't panic. Turn the machine on at once and the programme should start.

If there was a power cut and the bread was left for longer than just a few minutes you may need to discard the mixture, depending on where it was in the programme.

My kneader blade is stuck in the bread pan after baking. How can I get it out?

This often happens, especially if you have been using your machine a lot. Soak the bread pan in warm water with a little washing-up liquid for a few hours. Then, if it still won't move, bend a flexible spatula under the kneader blade to prise it off.

Can I put the bread pan in the dishwasher?

Sadly, no. Soak the pan in warm water with a little washing-up liquid, then give it a quick swish with a washing-up brush. Avoid scouring pads, which will scratch the nonstick coating.

Why has the bread stuck to the roof of the bread machine?

There is probably too much mixture for the size of the tin. Check with the manufacturer's handbook and scale down the quantity of ingredients.

You might have added too much yeast. Make sure you use proper measuring spoons, not ordinary spoons from the kitchen drawer. You must make sure that the spoon measures are level, not rounded.

If you have adapted a recipe reduce the quantities still further, including additional flavouring ingredients.

Some bread machine manufacturers specify warm water, others cold. Check the handbook.

Why has the top sunk?

Too much water. Always measure carefully.

Did you forget to add salt? Salt is needed to help control the rate at which yeast ferments, which, in turn, strengthens the gluten and stops the bread from rising too much and then collapsing.

It could be that the lid of the machine was not properly shut or that it was opened during the baking process.

Why is the crust so dark?

Double-check the crust setting and adjust to low next time.

Bake sweet breads on a sweet setting rather than on a basic white setting because the cooking temperature is slightly lower, so preventing an over-brown crust.

It's possible that the proportions of sugar and butter were too high. Refer to the handbook and reduce the amounts if necessary.

Reduce the amount of butter or cheese in savoury breads.

Why is the top of the bread very pale?

Wheat- and gluten-free breads tend to have very pale tops. Rectify this by brushing the baked bread with a little butter and then browning it for a few minutes under a preheated grill.

You might have left the crust setting on the palest setting. Adjust to medium or dark next time.

What has made the top of the bread so sticky?

The bread was left in the machine for too long after baking and the keep-warm facility had finished, so that the steam from the just cooked bread could not escape and so collected on the roof of the machine and then condensed back on to the bread.

Whenever possible remove the baked bread from the bread pan once the programme has finished.

Why are there large holes in the crumb?

You have added too much yeast.

Alternatively, you added too much water, or, if you were using warm water, the water was too hot and so killed the yeast. The water should be between 21 and 28°C (70–82°F) – that is, it should feel just warm or tepid to the touch.

It's possible that there was too much acid in the mixture, perhaps from yogurt, soured cream, buttermilk or fresh orange or lemon juice.

Why has the bread got a very close texture?

It could be that there was not enough yeast. Measure carefully.

If there was insufficient liquid the bread would be unable to stretch as the yeast expanded.

Everyday classics

Simple white loaf

This is a good family favourite. Put everything in the bread machine the night before, set the timer and wake up to the fabulous aroma of freshly baked bread in the morning ... what a way to begin the day!

Makes 750 g (1½ lb) loaf
Time 2 hours 50 minutes–
4 hours, *depending on machine*

275 ml (9 fl oz) water

2 tablespoons butter, at room temperature

1 teaspoon salt

475 g (15 oz) strong white flour, plus extra to finish

2 teaspoons caster sugar

1¼ teaspoons fast-action dried yeast

1 Lift the bread pan out of the bread machine and fit the kneader blade. Add the water, butter and salt. Spoon in the flour, make a slight dip in the centre and add the sugar and yeast.

2 Insert the pan into the bread machine. Shut the lid and set to a 750 g (1½ lb) loaf on a basic white setting with preferred crust setting. Press start.

3 At the end of the programme, lift the pan out of the machine using oven gloves. Loosen the bread with a plastic spatula and turn it out on to a wire rack. Sprinkle the top with a little extra flour and leave to cool.

Tip For a richer crust, add 2 tablespoons dried milk powder along with the sugar.

Honey and oat bread

For those who are not keen on brown bread this is a good halfway version made with white and wholemeal flours and speckled with porridge oats for an added fibre boost.

Makes 750 g (1½ lb) loaf
Time 1 hour–1 hour 10 minutes, *depending on machine*

275 ml (9 fl oz) warm water

2 tablespoons butter, at room temperature

1 teaspoon salt

200 g (7 oz) strong white flour

250 g (8 oz) strong wholemeal flour

50 g (2 oz) porridge oats

1 tablespoon set honey

2¾ teaspoons fast-action dried yeast

1 Lift the bread pan out of the bread machine and fit the kneader blade. Add the water, butter and salt. Spoon in the flours and oats, make a slight dip in the centre and add the honey and yeast.

2 Insert the pan into the bread machine. Shut the lid and set to a 750 g (1½ lb) loaf on a fastbake or rapid setting. Press start.

3 At the end of the programme, lift the pan out of the machine using oven gloves. Loosen the bread with a plastic spatula, turn it out on to a wire rack and leave to cool.

Tip If you don't have any honey, add light or dark muscovado sugar instead.

Healthy white bread

If anyone in your family won't eat brown bread, sneak some vitamins and protein past them in the form of wheatgerm and quinoa flakes.

Makes 750 g (1½ lb) loaf
Time 1 hour–1 hour
10 minutes, *depending on machine*

275 ml (9 fl oz) warm water

2 tablespoons sunflower oil

1 teaspoon salt

400 g (13 oz) strong white flour

40 g (1½ oz) toasted wheatgerm

50 g (2 oz) quinoa flakes

1 tablespoon set honey

2½ teaspoons fast-action dried yeast

1 Lift the bread pan out of the bread machine and fit the kneader blade. Add the water, oil and salt. Spoon in the flour, wheatgerm and quinoa flakes, make a slight dip in the centre and add the honey and yeast.

2 Insert the pan into the bread machine. Shut the lid and set to a 750 g (1½ lb) loaf on a fastbake or rapid setting. Press start.

3 At the end of the programme lift the pan out of the machine using oven gloves. Loosen the bread with a plastic spatula, turn it out on to a wire rack and leave to cool.

Note Wheatgerm, which is rich in vitamin E and folic acid, comes from the heart of the wheatgrain. Quinoa is one of the few cereals that contain all eight amino acids, so it is a valuable source of protein. It is sold as grains, flakes and in ground form.

Malted barley bread

This is a rough-textured, craggy bread, topped with extra barley flakes; it is made with malted barley extract and has a moist, rich flavour without the overpowering flavour that treacle can give.

Makes 750 g (1½ lb) loaf
Time 3½–5 hours, *depending on machine*

275 ml (9 fl oz) cold water

2 tablespoons milk powder

2 tablespoons butter, at room temperature

2 tablespoons malted barley extract

1 teaspoon salt

475 g (15 oz) malthouse flour

50 g (2 oz) barley flakes, plus extra to finish

1 tablespoon light muscovado sugar

1¼ teaspoon fast-action dried yeast

1 tablespoon fresh milk, to glaze

1 Lift the bread pan out of the bread machine and fit the kneader blade. Add the water, milk powder, butter, barley extract and salt. Spoon the flour and barley flakes over the top, make a slight dip in the centre and sprinkle in the sugar and yeast.

2 Insert the pan into the bread machine, shut the lid and set to a 750 g (1½ lb) loaf on a wholewheat setting with medium crust. Press start.

3 Just before baking begins, brush the dough with fresh milk and sprinkle with a few extra barley flakes. Gently and quickly shut the lid and leave to bake.

4 At the end of the programme, lift the pan out of the bread machine using oven gloves. Loosen the bread with a plastic spatula, turn it out on to a wire rack and leave to cool.

Tip Malted barley extract, which is most easily found in glass jars in health food stores, looks rather like slightly lighter coloured treacle.

Milk and muscovado bread

Adding milk to a loaf produces a rich golden crust and light crumb. If you prefer, use fresh milk instead of the water and milk powder but do not set the delay timer programme.

Makes 750 g (1½ lb) loaf
Time 2 hours 50 minutes–4 hours, *depending on machine*

275 ml (9 fl oz) water

2 tablespoons milk powder

2 tablespoons butter, at room temperature

1 teaspoon salt

475 g (15 oz) strong white flour

2 teaspoons light muscovado sugar

1¼ teaspoons fast-action dried yeast

1 Lift the bread pan out of the bread machine and fit the kneader blade. Add the water, milk powder, butter and salt. Spoon in the flour, make a slight dip in the centre and add the sugar and yeast.

2 Insert the pan into the bread machine, shut the lid and set to 750 g (1½ lb) loaf on a basic white setting with preferred crust setting. Press start.

3 At the end of the programme, lift the pan out of the machine using oven gloves. Loosen the bread with a plastic spatula, turn it out on to a wire rack and leave to cool.

Wholemeal spelt bread

Milled since Roman times, spelt is lower in gluten than other wheat flours, making it a possible choice for those who find other wheat flours difficult to digest. Look out, too, for white spelt flour.

Makes 750 g (1½ lb) loaf
Time 3½–5 hours, *depending on machine*

250 ml (8 fl oz) water

2 tablespoons sunflower oil

1 teaspoon salt

500 g (1 lb) wholemeal spelt flour, plus extra to finish

1 tablespoon light muscovado sugar

1¼ teaspoons fast-action dried yeast

1 tablespoon milk, to glaze

spelt flakes, to finish

1 Lift the bread pan out of the bread machine and fit the kneader blade. Add the water, oil and salt. Spoon in the flour, make a slight dip in the centre and add the sugar and yeast.

2 Insert the pan into the bread machine. Shut the lid and set to a 750 g (1½ lb) loaf on a wholewheat setting with preferred crust setting. Press start.

3 Just before baking begins, brush the top of the bread lightly with milk and sprinkle with the spelt flakes. Close the lid gently.

4 At the end of the programme lift the pan out of the machine using oven gloves. Loosen the bread with a plastic spatula, turn it out on to a wire rack and leave to cool.

Tip If you forget to brush the bread with milk and add spelt flakes, then dust with a little extra flour at the end of baking.

Speedy sesame bread

If you've just discovered that you have run out of bread, this speedy, one-rise version made with extra yeast can be on the table in around an hour.

Makes 750 g (1½ lb) loaf
Time 1 hour–1 hour 10 minutes, *depending on machine*

275 ml (9 fl oz) warm water

2 tablespoons milk powder

2 tablespoons sunflower oil

2 tablespoons sesame seeds

1 teaspoon salt

475 g (15 oz) strong white flour

1 tablespoon caster sugar

2½ teaspoons fast-action dried yeast

To finish

small knob of butter

a few sesame seeds

1 Lift the bread pan out of the bread machine and fit the kneader blade. Add the warm water, milk powder, oil, sesame seeds and salt. Spoon in the flour, make a slight dip in the centre and add the sugar and yeast.

2 Insert the pan into the bread machine. Shut the lid and set to 750 g (1½ lb) fastbake or rapid setting. Press start.

3 At the end of the programme, lift the pan out of the machine using oven gloves. Loosen the bread with a plastic spatula and turn it out on to a wire rack. Brush the top of the loaf with the butter and sprinkle with a few extra sesame seeds. Brown under the grill if liked.

Tip Not all bread machines have a fastbake or rapid setting, so double-check with the manufacturer's handbook before you begin. As this programme is so fast, warm water is needed, and the programme can be set to only one crust option.

Enriched white loaf

This large, white loaf has a light, open texture, similar to a brioche. It's a good, all-purpose bread, ideal served warm or toasted with butter or jam or made into sandwiches.

Makes 750 g (1½ lb) loaf
Time 2 hours 50 minutes–4 hours, *depending on machine*

1 egg

1 egg yolk

2 tablespoons butter, at room temperature

200 ml (7 fl oz) milk

1 teaspoon salt

475 g (15 oz) strong white flour

1 tablespoon caster sugar

1 teaspoon fast-action dried yeast

1 Lift the bread pan out of the bread machine and fit the kneader blade. Add the whole egg, egg yolk, butter, milk and salt. Spoon in the flour, make a slight dip in the centre and add the sugar and yeast.

2 Insert the pan into the bread machine. Shut the lid and set to a 750 g (1½ lb) loaf on a basic white setting with preferred crust setting. Press start.

3 At the end of the programme, lift the pan out of the machine using oven gloves. Loosen the bread with a plastic spatula, turn it out on to a wire rack and leave to cool.

Note Do not use the delay timer programme with this recipe because it contains eggs and milk.

Semolina and olive oil bread

Based on a North African bread, this rustic-style loaf is made with a high proportion of olive oil and a blend of ground semolina and strong white flour for a more unusually textured bread.

Makes 750 g (1½ lb) loaf
Time 2 hours 50 minutes–4 hours, *depending on machine*

200 ml (7 fl oz) water

6 tablespoons olive oil

1 teaspoon salt

150 g (5 oz) finely ground semolina

300 g (10 oz) strong white flour

2 teaspoons caster sugar

1¼ teaspoons fast-action dried yeast

1 Lift the bread pan out of the bread machine and fit the kneader blade. Add the water, oil and salt. Spoon in the semolina and flour, make a slight dip in the centre and add the sugar and yeast.

2 Insert the pan into the bread machine. Shut the lid and set to a 750 g (1½ lb) loaf on a basic white setting with preferred crust setting. Press start.

3 At the end of the programme, lift the pan out of the machine using oven gloves. Loosen the bread with a plastic spatula, turn it out on to a wire rack and leave to cool.

Tip Traditionally, this bread would be shaped into a large, round, shallow bread. If you prefer, set the bread to dough only, then knead, shape and allow to rise on a baking sheet. Brush with egg yolk glaze, sprinkle with sesame seeds and bake in a preheated oven, 200°C (400°F), Gas Mark 6, for 25–30 minutes.

Multigrain wholemeal bread

This blend of five different ground and flaked grains produces a healthy, slightly closer textured bread with just a hint of rye. Try toasting it and topping with grilled tomatoes drizzled with a little balsamic vinegar.

Makes 750 g (1½ lb) loaf
Time 3½–5 hours, *depending on machine*

300 ml (½ pint) water

2 tablespoons sunflower oil

1½ teaspoons salt

25 g (1 oz) medium oatmeal, plus extra to finish

25 g (1 oz) barley flakes, plus extra to finish

25 g (1 oz) quinoa flakes

100 g (3½ oz) rye flour

375 g (12 oz) strong wholemeal flour with malted wheat grains

2 tablespoons dark muscovado sugar

1¼ teaspoons fast-action dried yeast

1 tablespoon milk, to finish

1 Lift the bread pan out of the bread machine and fit the kneader blade. Add the water, oil and salt. Spoon in the oatmeal, barley and quinoa flakes, then add the flours. Make a slight dip in the centre and add the sugar and yeast.

2 Insert the pan into the bread machine. Shut the lid and set to a 750 g (1½ lb) loaf on a wholewheat setting with preferred crust setting. Press start.

3 Just before baking begins, brush with a little milk and sprinkle with extra oatmeal and barley flakes. Close the lid gently.

4 At the end of the programme, lift the pan out of the machine using oven gloves. Loosen the bread with a plastic spatula, turn it out on to a wire rack and leave to cool.

Tip Oatmeal is thought to help reduce blood cholesterol, while barley soothes digestion and quinoa adds a protein boost.

Rapid light granary bread

In most bread machines there is a rapid or fastbake programme for white bread only, but using a combination of white and granary flours with an extra boost of yeast will give a light brown loaf with a good, open texture.

Makes 750 g (1½ lb) loaf
Time 1 hour–1 hour 10 minutes, *depending on machine*

275 ml (9 fl oz) warm water

2 tablespoons sunflower oil

1½ teaspoons salt

275 g (9 oz) strong granary flour, plus extra to finish (optional)

200 g (7 oz) strong white flour, plus extra to finish (optional)

1 tablespoon dark muscovado sugar

2¾ teaspoons fast-action dried yeast

1 Lift the bread pan out of the bread machine and fit the kneader blade. Add the warm water, oil and salt. Spoon in the flours, make a slight dip in the centre and add the sugar and yeast.

2 Insert the pan into the bread machine. Shut the lid and set to 750 g (1½ lb) fastbake or rapid setting. Press start.

3 At the end of the programme, lift the pan out of the machine using oven gloves. Loosen the bread with a plastic spatula and turn it out on to a wire rack. Sprinkle the top of the loaf with a little extra flour, if liked.

Tip Because wholewheat loaves usually take longer to rise than white ones in the bread machine, more yeast has been added than in an all-white fastbake recipe to compensate for the reduced time in the machine.

Traditional wholewheat bread

This classic wholewheat loaf is flavoured with treacle and a little toasted wheatgerm. If you can't find malthouse flour in your local supermarket, use granary instead.

Makes 750 g (1½ lb) loaf
Time 3½–5 hours, *depending on machine*

300 ml (½ pint) cold water

2 tablespoons butter, at room temperature

1 teaspoon salt

425 g (14 oz) strong malthouse flour

40 g (1½ oz) toasted wheatgerm

¼ plain or orange-flavoured 1000 mg vitamin C tablet

1 tablespoon black treacle

1¼ teaspoons fast-action dried yeast

1 Lift the bread pan out of the bread machine and fit the kneader blade. Add the water, butter and salt. Spoon in the flour and wheatgerm and make a slight dip in the centre. Crush the vitamin C tablet between 2 teaspoons and add it to the flour with the treacle and yeast.

2 Insert the pan into the bread machine. Shut the lid and set to a 750 g (1½ lb) loaf on a wholewheat setting with preferred crust setting. Press start.

3 At the end of the programme, lift the pan out of the machine using oven gloves. Loosen the bread with a plastic spatula, turn it out on to a wire rack and leave to cool.

Tip The longer your bread machine programme takes, the lighter the finished loaf will be.

Note If using the delay timer programme, keep the treacle and yeast separate.

Light wholemeal bread with omega boosters

This healthy bread is rich in omega-3 and omega-6 fatty acids, thought to aid brain development and growth, to keep our immune system healthy and to help to reduce inflammation in people with arthritis.

Makes 750 g (1½ lb) loaf
Time 1 hour–1 hour 10 minutes, *depending on machine*

275 ml (9 fl oz) warm water

2 tablespoons sunflower oil

1 teaspoon salt

200 g (7 oz) strong malthouse flour

200 g (7 oz) strong white flour

25 g (1 oz) hemp flour

1 tablespoon light muscovado sugar

2¾ teaspoons fast-action dried yeast

50 g (2 oz) unblanched almonds, roughly chopped

50 g (2 oz) dried cranberries

3 tablespoons pumpkin seeds

3 tablespoons golden linseeds

1 Lift the bread pan out of the bread machine and fit the kneader blade. Add the warm water, oil and salt. Spoon in the flours, make a slight dip in the centre and add the sugar and yeast. Spoon the almonds, cranberries and seeds on top.

2 Insert the pan into the bread machine. Shut the lid and set to a 750 g (1½ lb) loaf on a fastbake or rapid setting. Press start.

3 At the end of the programme, lift the pan out of the machine using oven gloves. Loosen the bread with a plastic spatula, turn it out on to a wire rack and leave to cool.

Tip Sesame and sunflower seeds could also be used with the pumpkin seeds and linseeds if available, adding 1½–2 tablespoons of each kind of seed, just as long as you have a total of 6 tablespoons in all.

Light seeded wholemeal bread

If you are making this for someone who is not very keen on seeds, finely chop or grind them in a liquidizer before adding them to the bread pan.

Makes 750 g (1½ lb) loaf
Time 2 hours 50 minutes–
4 hours, *depending on machine*

275 ml (9 fl oz) water

2 tablespoons milk powder

2 tablespoons sunflower oil

1 teaspoon salt

25 g (1 oz) pumpkin seeds,
plus extra to finish

25 g (1 oz) sunflower seeds,
plus extra to finish

2 tablespoons golden linseeds,
plus extra to finish

275 g (9 oz) strong wholemeal flour

200 g (7 oz) strong white flour

1 tablespoon light muscovado sugar

1¼ teaspoons fast-action
dried yeast

1 tablespoon milk to glaze

1 Lift the bread pan out of the bread machine and fit the kneader blade. Add the water, milk powder, oil and salt. Spoon in the seeds and flours, make a slight dip in the centre and add the sugar and yeast.

2 Insert the pan into the bread machine. Shut the lid and set to a 750 g (1½ lb) loaf on a basic white setting with preferred crust setting. Press start.

3 Just before baking begins, brush the top of the loaf with milk and sprinkle with extra seeds.

4 At the end of the programme, lift the pan out of the machine using oven gloves. Loosen the bread with a plastic spatula, turn it out on to a wire rack and leave to cool.

Tip For a crisp crust, mix 2 teaspoons salt with 2 tablespoons water and brush this over the top of the loaf instead of the milk.

Gourmet breads

Beer and brown sugar bread

A good talking point, this coarse rustic loaf is made with Guinness or stout and dark muscovado sugar, and it is lovely served warm, torn into chunky pieces and eaten with soft Bleu d'Auvergne or Manchego cheese.

Makes 750 g (1½ lb) loaf
Time 3½–5 hours, *depending on machine*

200 ml (7 fl oz) Guinness or strong brown beer

100 ml (3½ fl oz) cold water

2 tablespoons sunflower oil

1 teaspoon salt

100 g (3½ oz) rye flour

375 g (12 oz) strong granary flour

2 tablespoons dark muscovado sugar

1¼ teaspoons fast-action dried yeast

To finish

1 tablespoon milk

1 tablespoon poppy seeds

1 Lift the bread pan out of the bread machine and fit the kneader blade. Add the beer, water, oil and salt. Spoon in the flours, make a slight dip in the centre and add the sugar and yeast.

2 Insert the pan into the bread machine. Shut the lid and set to a 750 g (1½ lb) loaf on a wholewheat setting with preferred crust setting. Press start.

3 Just before baking begins, brush the top of the bread with the milk and sprinkle with the poppy seeds. Gently and quickly shut the lid and continue the programme.

4 At the end of the programme, lift the pan out of the machine using oven gloves. Loosen the bread with a plastic spatula, turn it out on to a wire rack and leave to cool.

Tip If you only have a paler beer or lager, use 300 ml (½ pint) and omit the water.

Fennel and buttermilk bread

Adding buttermilk to granary bread produces a light, airy bread without the need for extra yeast or vitamin C. Flavoured with just a hint of crushed fennel seeds, this bread is ideal for sandwiches or toast.

Makes 750 g (1½ lb) loaf
Time 3½–5 hours, *depending on machine*

125 ml (4 fl oz) water

150 ml (¼ pint) buttermilk

1 teaspoon salt

3 teaspoons fennel seeds, roughly crushed

475 g (15 oz) strong granary flour, plus extra to finish

2 teaspoons light muscovado sugar

1¼ teaspoons fast-action dried yeast

1 Lift the bread pan out of the bread machine and fit the kneader blade. Add the water, buttermilk, salt and fennel seeds. Spoon in the flour, make a slight dip in the centre and add the sugar and yeast.

2 Insert the pan into the bread machine. Shut the lid and set to a 750 g (1½ lb) loaf on a wholewheat setting with preferred crust setting. Press start.

3 At the end of the programme, lift the pan out of the machine using oven gloves. Loosen the bread with a plastic spatula and turn it out on to a wire rack. Dust the top with a little extra flour and leave to cool.

Tip If you don't have a pestle and mortar to crush the fennel seeds, put them into a mug and use the end of a rolling pin.

Note Do not use the delay timer programme with this recipe.

Mediterranean herb bread

A versatile loaf, this bread is equally good served warm with bowls of steaming hot soup, with barbecues and salad, or made into sandwiches and filled with ham or cheese.

Makes 750 g (1½ lb) loaf
Time 2 hours 50 minutes–
4 hours, *depending on machine*

275 ml (9 fl oz) cold water

2 tablespoons olive oil, plus extra to finish

1 teaspoon salt

1 teaspoon dried oregano

3 stems of rosemary, leaves stripped from stems, finely chopped

handful of basil leaves, roughly chopped

2 fresh or dried lavender flowers, crumbled (optional)

475 g (15 oz) strong white flour

1 teaspoon caster sugar

1¼ teaspoons fast-action dried yeast

a few coarse salt flakes, to finish

1 Lift the bread pan out of the bread machine and fit the kneader blade. Add the water, oil and salt. Sprinkle in the dried and fresh herbs and add the lavender (if using). Spoon in the flour, make a slight dip in the centre and add the sugar and yeast.

2 Insert the pan into the bread machine. Shut the lid and set to a 750 g (1½ lb) loaf on a basic white setting with preferred crust setting. Press start.

3 At the end of the programme, lift the pan out of the machine using oven gloves. Loosen the bread with a plastic spatula, turn it out on to a wire rack, brush the top with a little extra oil and sprinkle with some coarse salt.

Tip If the top of the bread is paler than you would like, brown it under the grill after adding the oil and salt.

Lemon, dill and soured cream bread

Moist and delicately flavoured, this bread is the perfect base for smoked salmon open sandwiches or filled with tuna and salad for a more everyday lunch. If you don't have any dill use fresh tarragon.

Makes 750 g (1½ lb) loaf
Time 3½–5 hours, *depending on machine*

200 ml (7 fl oz) cold water

grated rind of 1 lemon

150 g (5 oz) full-fat crème fraîche

1 teaspoon salt

½ teaspoon coarsely crushed black peppercorns

2 tablespoons chopped dill

2 tablespoons chopped parsley

500 g (1 lb) strong wholemeal flour

1 teaspoon caster sugar

1¼ teaspoons fast-action dried yeast

1 Lift the bread pan out of the bread machine and fit the kneader blade. Add the water, lemon rind and crème fraîche. Spoon in the salt, pepper and herbs, then the flour. Make a slight dip in the centre and add the sugar and yeast.

2 Insert the pan into the bread machine. Shut the lid and set to a 750 g (1½ lb) loaf on a wholewheat setting with preferred crust setting. Press start.

3 At the end of the programme, lift the pan out of the machine using oven gloves. Loosen the bread with a plastic spatula, turn it out on to a wire rack and leave to cool.

Note Because this bread contains crème fraîche, do not use the delay timer programme but begin mixing, rising and baking immediately.

Celery and walnut bread with buckwheat

Just a small amount of buckwheat flour will add a delicious nuttiness to any bread. Mixed with walnut pieces and diced celery, it makes this bread the ideal accompaniment to serve ploughman's lunch style.

Makes 750 g (1½ lb) loaf
Time 3½–5 hours, *depending on machine*

275 ml (9 fl oz) water

2 tablespoons olive oil

1 teaspoon salt

50 g (2 oz) walnut pieces, plus extra to finish

1 teaspoon celery seeds (optional)

2 celery sticks, diced

75 g (3 oz) buckwheat flour

375 g (12 oz) strong wholemeal flour

¼ plain or orange-flavoured 1000 mg vitamin C tablet

1 tablespoon light muscovado sugar

1½ teaspoons fast-action dried yeast

fresh milk, to finish

1 Lift the bread pan out of the bread machine and fit the kneader blade. Add the water, oil, salt, walnut pieces, celery seeds (if using) and celery. Spoon in the flours and make a slight dip in the centre. Crush the vitamin C tablet between 2 teaspoons and add with the sugar and yeast.

2 Insert the pan into the bread machine. Shut the lid and set to a 750 g (1½ lb) loaf on a wholewheat setting with preferred crust setting. Press start.

3 Just before baking begins, brush the top of the bread with a little milk and sprinkle with some extra walnut pieces.

4 At the end of the programme, lift the pan out of the bread machine using oven gloves. Loosen the bread with a plastic spatula, turn it out on to a wire rack and leave to cool.

Tip The longer the wholewheat cycle is on your machine, the lighter your bread will be.

Five-seed wholewheat bread

A nutty-tasting granary bread that will boost your daily intake of vitamin E and of B vitamins, minerals and fibre, which are thought to help reduce blood cholesterol. Delicious toasted and spread with jam.

Makes 750 g (1½ lb) loaf
Time 3½–5 hours, *depending on machine*

300 ml (½ pint) cold water

2 tablespoons butter, at room temperature

2 tablespoons milk powder

1½ teaspoons salt

475 g (15 oz) granary flour

2 tablespoons pumpkin seeds

2 tablespoons sunflower seeds

2 tablespoons sesame seeds

2 tablespoons linseeds

2 tablespoons poppy seeds

¼ plain or orange-flavoured 1000 mg vitamin C tablet

1 tablespoon light muscovado sugar

1¼ teaspoons fast-action dried yeast

To finish

fresh milk

extra seeds

1 Lift the bread pan out of the bread machine and fit the kneader blade. Add the water, butter, milk powder and salt. Spoon in the flour and seeds. Crush the vitamin C tablet between 2 teaspoons and add to pan. Make a slight dip in the flour and add the sugar and yeast.

2 Insert the pan into the bread machine. Shut the lid and set to 750 g (1½ lb) loaf on a wholewheat setting with preferred crust setting. Press start.

3 Just before baking begins, brush the top of the loaf with a little fresh milk and sprinkle with some extra seeds. Close the lid gently.

4 At the end of the programme, lift the pan out of the bread machine using oven gloves. Loosen the bread with a plastic spatula, turn it out on to a wire rack and leave to cool.

Tip Vary the seeds depending on what you have, adding more or less of one kind or another, reducing the types of seeds or even adding different ones, such as hemp seeds. Just make sure that you don't use more than 100 g (3½ oz) in total.

Caramelized red onion and red Leicester bread

This versatile bread is ideal served with soups, salads or made into sandwiches. Red Leicester cheese adds a deep orange colour and a mild cheesy flavour to the bread, for a stronger taste use Cheddar instead.

Makes 750 g (1½ lb) loaf
Time 2 hours 50 minutes–4 hours, *depending on machine*

1 tablespoon olive oil

1 red onion, thinly sliced

3 teaspoons caster sugar

250 ml (8 fl oz) water

1 teaspoon salt

1 teaspoon English mustard, ready made or powder

½ teaspoon peppercorns, roughly crushed

100 g (3½ oz) red Leicester cheese, grated

425 g (14 oz) strong white flour

1¼ teaspoons fast-action dried yeast

1 Heat the oil in a frying pan, add the onion and fry over a medium heat for 5 minutes until softened. Sprinkle with 1 teaspoon of the sugar and fry for 5 more minutes until the onion is lightly caramelized. Leave to cool.

2 Lift the pan out of the bread machine and fit the kneader blade. Add the water, salt, mustard, peppercorns and cheese. Spoon in the flour, make a slight dip in the centre and add the remaining sugar and yeast.

3 Insert the pan into the bread machine. Shut the lid and set to a 750 g (1½ lb) loaf on a basic white setting with a pale crust setting. Press start.

4 When the raisin beep sounds, gradually add the onions.

5 At the end of the programme, lift the pan out of the machine using oven gloves. Loosen the bread with a plastic spatula, turn it out on to a wire rack and leave to cool.

Tip Because this bread has a higher proportion of cheese than other breads it will produce a darker crust. If your machine does not have a setting for crust colour, set the machine to sweet breads, which will have a lower baking temperature.

Buckwheat, cranberry and pomegranate bread

Buckwheat flour adds a rich, earthy, rather bitter flavour, and because it has such a strong taste a little goes a long way. The ruby-red dried cranberries and pomegranate seeds complement slightly acidic cheeses.

Makes 750 g (1½ lb) loaf
Time 2 hours 50 minutes–4 hours, *depending on machine*

300 ml (½ pint) cold water

2 tablespoons olive oil

1 teaspoon salt

3 tablespoons dried pomegranate seeds

125 g (4 oz) buckwheat flour, plus extra to finish

375 g (12 oz) strong white flour

1 tablespoon light muscovado sugar

1¼ teaspoons fast-action dried yeast

75 g (3 oz) dried cranberries

1 Lift the bread pan out of the bread machine and fit the kneader blade. Add the water, oil, salt and pomegranate seeds. Spoon in the flours, make a slight dip in the centre and add the sugar and yeast.

2 Insert the pan into the bread machine. Shut the lid and set to a 750 g (1½ lb) loaf on a basic white setting with preferred crust setting. Press start.

3 At the end of the programme, lift the pan out of the machine using oven gloves. Loosen the bread with a plastic spatula, turn it out on to a wire rack, dust the top lightly with a little extra flour and leave to cool.

Tip Despite is name, buckwheat flour is wheat free and as such contains only low amounts of gluten, so mix it with wheat flours for a well-risen loaf.

Pesto and marinated olive bread

The better flavoured the olives you use, the more intense the flavour of the finished bread will be, so choose olives from the deli counter in your local supermarket but make sure that they are pitted.

Makes 750 ml (1½ lb) loaf
Time 2 hours 50 minutes–
4 hours, *depending on machine*

200 ml (7 fl oz) water

2 tablespoons olive oil

2 tablespoons pesto

1 teaspoon salt

425 g (14 oz) strong white flour

1 teaspoon caster sugar

1¼ teaspoons fast-action dried yeast

125 g (4 oz) pitted and marinated mixed olives, halved

1 Lift the bread pan out of the bread machine and fit the kneader blade. Add the water, oil, pesto and salt. Spoon in the flour, make a slight dip in the centre and add the sugar and yeast.

2 Insert the pan into the bread machine. Shut the lid and set to a 750 g (1½ lb) loaf on a basic white setting with preferred crust setting. Press start.

3 When the raisin beep sounds, gradually add the olives.

4 At the end of the programme, lift the pan out of the machine using oven gloves. Loosen the bread with a plastic spatula, turn it out on to a wire rack and leave to cool.

Tip Don't be tempted to add the olives all in one go or you will jam the kneader blade and stop it from going round.

Hemp and sunflower seed bread

Rich in omega-6 oils, hemp flour is a healthy addition to any bread recipe, although its dark green colour can be a little surprising the first time you use it. Reminiscent of German breads, it stales slowly.

Makes 750 g (1½ lb) loaf
Time 3½–5 hours, *depending on machine*

300 ml (½ pint) water

2 tablespoons olive oil

1½ teaspoons salt

50 g (2 oz) sunflower seeds

50 g (2 oz) hemp flour

425 g (14 oz) malthouse bread flour or strong wholemeal flour with malted grains

¼ plain or orange-flavoured 1000 mg vitamin C tablet

1 tablespoon set honey

1¼ teaspoons fast-action dried yeast

To finish

fresh milk

a few hemp and sunflower seeds

1 Lift the bread pan out of the bread machine and fit the kneader blade. Add the water, oil, salt and sunflower seeds. Spoon in the flours and make a slight dip in the centre. Crush the vitamin C tablet between 2 teaspoons and add with the honey and yeast.

2 Insert the pan into the bread machine. Shut the lid and set to a 750 g (1½ lb) loaf on a wholewheat setting with preferred crust setting. Press start.

3 Just before baking, brush the loaf with a little milk and sprinkle with a few extra seeds, if liked.

4 At the end of the programme, lift the pan out of the machine using oven gloves. Loosen the bread with a plastic spatula, turn it out on to a wire rack and leave to cool.

Tip Buy hemp flour and hemp seeds from your local health food shop.

Note If using the delay timer programme, keep the vitamin C, honey and yeast separate.

Indian spiced chickpea bread

This light, golden-yellow bread is speckled with curry spices and mashed chickpeas; it is a good way to add fibre to bread without the family really realizing. Serve warm with curries or lentil-based soups.

Makes 750 g (1½ lb) loaf
Time 2 hours 50 minutes–4 hours, *depending on machine*

410 g (13½ oz) can chickpeas, drained, rinsed and roughly mashed

250 ml (8 fl oz) water

2 tablespoons mild curry paste

3 teaspoons black onion seeds

1 teaspoon coriander seeds, roughly crushed

1 teaspoon cumin seeds, roughly crushed

1½ teaspoons salt

425 g (14 oz) strong white flour

2 teaspoons caster sugar

1¼ teaspoons fast-action dried yeast

1 Lift the bread pan out of the bread machine and fit the kneader blade. Add the chickpeas, water, curry paste, onion seeds, crushed coriander and cumin seeds and salt. Spoon in the flour, make a slight dip in the centre and add the sugar and yeast.

2 Insert the pan into the bread machine. Shut the lid and set to a 750 g (1½ lb) basic white setting with preferred crust setting. Press start.

3 At the end of the programme, lift the pan out of the machine using oven gloves. Loosen the bread with a plastic spatula, turn it out on to a wire rack and leave to cool.

Tip Tikka masala or korma curry paste can be used or, for a slightly hotter taste, add rogan josh paste.

Chilli and sun-dried tomato bread

This light, open-textured bread is flavoured with a mix of smoked paprika and fresh chilli for a mellow but spicy heat. Serve warm with steaming bowls of soup or transform cheese on toast into something more exotic.

Makes 750 g (1½ lb) loaf
Time 2 hours 50 minutes–4 hours, *depending on machine*

275 ml (9 fl oz) cold water

2 tablespoons olive oil

1 teaspoon salt

1 teaspoon smoked paprika

1 large mild fresh red chilli, halved, deseeded and finely chopped

300 g (10 oz) strong white flour

150 g (5 oz) strong wholemeal flour

1 teaspoon caster sugar

1¼ teaspoons fast-action dried yeast

50 g (2 oz) sun-dried tomatoes in oil, drained and roughly chopped (optional)

1 Lift the bread pan out of the bread machine and fit the kneader blade. Add the water, oil, salt, paprika and chopped chilli. Spoon in the flours, make a slight dip in the top and sprinkle in the sugar and yeast.

2 Insert the pan into the bread machine. Shut the lid and set to a 750 g (1½ lb) loaf on a basic white setting with preferred crust setting. Press start. When the raisin beep sounds, gradually add the sun-dried tomatoes (if using).

3 At the end of the programme lift the pan out of the machine using oven gloves. Loosen the bread with a plastic spatula, turn it out on to a wire rack and leave to cool.

Tip Save time and use 1–2 teaspoons of ready-chopped red chilli from a jar, depending on your taste.

Tarragon and ricotta bread

Lightly flavoured with fresh tarragon, this loaf lends itself to tuna fish sandwiches or as an accompaniment for salmon or smoked mackerel pâté.

Makes 750 g (1½ lb) loaf
Time 2 hours 50 minutes–
4 hours, *depending on machine*

250 ml (8 fl oz) water

150 g (5 oz) ricotta cheese

1 teaspoon salt

½ teaspoon mixed coloured peppercorns, roughly crushed

2 tablespoons chopped tarragon

200 g (7 oz) strong wholemeal flour

250 g (8 oz) strong white flour

1 teaspoon caster sugar

1¼ teaspoons fast-action dried yeast

4 spring onions, trimmed and chopped

1 Lift the bread pan out of the bread machine and fit the kneader blade. Add the water, ricotta, salt, peppercorns and tarragon. Spoon in the flours, make a slight dip in the centre and add the sugar and yeast.

2 Insert the pan into the bread machine. Shut the lid and set to a 750 g (1½ lb) loaf on a basic white setting with preferred crust setting. Press start.

3 When the raisin beep sounds, add the spring onions.

4 At the end of the programme, lift the pan out of the machine using oven gloves. Loosen the bread with a plastic spatula, turn it out on to a wire rack and leave to cool.

Tip Don't be tempted to use dried tarragon, which has a strong, overpowering flavour, even when the quantities are greatly reduced. If you can't get any fresh tarragon use fresh rosemary or thyme leaves instead.

Lager and mustard bread

Mixed with lager and English mustard, this bread rises well and has a rustic, craggy top and golden crusty exterior. Although the only liquid in the bread is lager, the bread has a surprisingly mild flavour.

Makes 750 g (1½ lb) loaf
Time 2 hours 50 minutes–4 hours, *depending on machine*

250 ml (8 fl oz) lager

2 tablespoons sunflower oil

3 teaspoons English mustard

1 teaspoon salt

200 g (7 oz) strong malthouse flour

250 g (8 oz) strong white flour

1 tablespoon light muscovado sugar

1¼ teaspoons fast-action dried yeast

1 Lift the bread pan out of the bread machine and fit the kneader blade. Add the lager, oil, mustard and salt. Spoon in the flours, make a slight dip in the centre and add the sugar and yeast.

2 Insert the pan into the bread machine. Shut the lid and set to a 750 g (1½ lb) loaf on a basic white setting with preferred crust setting. Press start.

3 At the end of the programme, lift the pan out of the machine using oven gloves. Loosen the bread with a plastic spatula, turn it out on to a wire rack and leave to cool.

Tip The same amount of German mustard can also be used. If you use Dijon or wholegrain mustard, which have a milder flavour, you will need to add 4 teaspoons.

Beetroot, horseradish and caraway bread

This vibrant coloured bread is an amazing deep pink and makes an eye-catching sandwich. It is delicious with smoked ham and salad or as an accompaniment for smooth, creamy vegetable soups.

Makes 750 g (1½ lb) loaf
Time 2 hours 50 minutes–4 hours, *depending on machine*

150 ml (¼ pint) cold water

200 g (7 oz) cooked and peeled beetroot in natural juices, drained and coarsely grated

1 tablespoon sunflower oil

1½ teaspoons salt

2 teaspoons hot horseradish sauce (from a jar)

1 teaspoon caraway seeds, roughly crushed

425 g (14 oz) strong white flour

2 teaspoons caster sugar

1¼ teaspoons fast-action dried yeast

1 Lift the bread pan out of the bread machine and fit the kneader blade. Add the water, grated beetroot, oil and salt, then the horseradish and caraway seeds. Spoon in the flour, make a slight dip in the centre and add the sugar and yeast.

2 Insert the pan into the bread machine. Shut the lid and set to a 750 g (1½ lb) loaf on a basic white setting with preferred crust setting. Press start.

3 At the end of the programme, lift the pan out of the machine using oven gloves. Loosen the bread with a plastic spatula, turn it out on to a wire rack and leave to cool.

Tip Choose vacuum packs of ready-cooked beetroot in natural juices rather then those in vinegar and make sure you drain them well before grating.

Date, sultana and hazelnut bread

Even if you don't have much time, you can still produce interestingly flavoured breads such as this crusty, nicely domed bread, using the fastbake or rapid setting. Just remember to use warm water and more yeast.

Makes 750 g (1½ lb) loaf
Time 1 hour–1 hour 10 minutes, *depending on machine*

275 ml (9 fl oz) warm water

2 tablespoons milk powder

2 tablespoons sunflower oil

1 teaspoon salt

25 g (1 oz) toasted wheatgerm

200 g (7 oz) strong wholemeal flour

200 g (7 oz) strong white flour

2 tablespoons dark muscovado sugar

2¾ teaspoons fast-action dried yeast

50 g (2 oz) hazelnuts, toasted and roughly chopped

100 g (3½ oz) pitted dates, sliced

75 g (3 oz) sultanas

1 Lift the bread pan out of the bread machine and fit the kneader blade. Add the warm water, milk powder, oil and salt. Spoon in the wheatgerm and flours, make a slight dip in the centre and spoon in the sugar and yeast. Top with the nuts, dates and sultanas.

2 Insert the pan into the bread machine. Shut the lid and set to a 750 g (1½ lb) loaf on a fastbake or rapid setting. Press start.

3 At the end of the programme, lift the pan out of the machine using oven gloves. Loosen the bread with a plastic spatula, turn it out on to a wire rack and leave to cool.

Tip Dried figs or dried apricots could be added in place of the dates if liked, or try adding untoasted pecans or almonds instead of the hazelnuts.

Note Do not set the delay timer programme for this recipe.

Rocket, feta and sun-dried tomato bread

Serve this deliciously flavoured golden bread while it's still warm with barbecued meats, pasta or bowls of steaming hot soup.

Makes 750 g (1½ lb) loaf
Time 2 hours 50 minutes–
4 hours, *depending on machine*

200 ml (7 fl oz) water

150 g (5 oz) feta cheese, crumbled into small pieces

2 tablespoons olive oil

1 teaspoon salt

400 g (13 oz) strong white flour

1 teaspoon caster sugar

1¼ teaspoons fast-action dried yeast

50 g (2 oz) sun-dried tomatoes in oil, drained and roughly chopped

50 g (2 oz) rocket leaves, roughly chopped

1 Lift the bread pan out of the bread machine and fit the kneader blade. Add the water, feta, oil and salt. Spoon in the flour, make a slight dip in the centre and add the sugar and yeast.

2 Insert the pan into the bread machine. Shut the lid and set to a 750 g (1½ lb) loaf on a basic white setting with a light crust setting. Press start.

3 When the raisin beep sounds, gradually add the tomatoes and rocket.

4 At the end of the programme, lift the pan out of the machine using oven gloves. Loosen the bread with a plastic spatula, turn it out on to a wire rack and leave to cool.

Tip Add the extra ingredients gradually so that the kneader blade does not get jammed. If it does, loosen the added ingredients in the corners of the bread pan with a plastic spatula.

Potato and wholegrain mustard bread

Adding just-cooked mashed potato produces a bread with a surprisingly light, fluffy texture. It's delicious served warm with soups; toast and top any leftovers with melting cheese and a drizzle of Worcestershire sauce.

Makes 750 g (1½ lb) loaf
Time 2 hours 50 minutes– 4 hours, *depending on machine*

250 g (8 oz) potato, peeled and cut into large chunks

150 ml (¼ pint) water

2 tablespoons butter, at room temperature

4 teaspoons wholegrain mustard

1 teaspoon salt

¼ teaspoon turmeric

¼ teaspoon cayenne pepper

425 g (14 oz) strong white flour

2 teaspoons caster sugar

1¼ teaspoons fast-action dried yeast

1 Cook the potato in a saucepan of boiling water for 15 minutes until just tender. Drain and mash, then leave to cool for 15 minutes.

2 Lift the pan out of the bread machine and fit the kneader blade. Add the mashed potato, water, butter, mustard, salt, turmeric and pepper. Spoon in the flour, make a slight dip in the centre and add the sugar and yeast.

3 Insert the pan into the bread machine. Shut the lid and set to a 750 g (1½ lb) loaf on a basic white setting with preferred crust setting. Press start.

4 At the end of the programme, lift the pan out of the machine using oven gloves. Loosen the bread with a plastic spatula, turn it out on to a wire rack and leave to cool.

Tip You can use 200 g (7 oz) cold leftover mashed potato, but it will produce a denser bread.

Rye and caraway bread

This dark, German-style bread tastes equally good spread with cream cheese and topped with smoked salmon, salad and smoked herrings, salad and smoked ham, or toasted and spread with apricot jam.

Makes 750 g (½ lb) loaf
Time 3½–5 hours, *depending on machine*

275 ml (9 fl oz) cold water

2 tablespoons milk powder

2 tablespoons sunflower oil

2 teaspoons caraway seeds

1 teaspoon salt

150 g (5 oz) rye flour

325 g (11 oz) strong malthouse flour

¼ plain or orange-flavoured 1000 mg vitamin C tablet

2 tablespoons black treacle

1¼ teaspoons fast-action dried yeast

1 Lift the bread pan out of the bread machine and fit the kneader blade. Add the water, milk powder, oil, caraway seeds and salt. Spoon in the flours and make a slight dip in the centre. Crush the vitamin C tablet between 2 teaspoons then add to the flour with the treacle and yeast.

2 Insert the pan into the bread machine. Shut the lid and set to a 750 g (1½ lb) loaf on a wholewheat setting with preferred crust setting. Press start.

3 At the end of the programme, lift the pan out of the machine using oven gloves. Loosen the bread with a plastic spatula, turn it out on to a wire rack and leave to cool.

Tip If you don't have any caraway seeds, simply leave them out.

Note If using the delay timer programme keep the vitamin C, treacle and yeast separate.

Chillied chocolate and fig bread

A rich, dark loaf, with just a hint of sweetness; serve this Mexican inspired bread with meaty beef or venison stews or try it at teatime with a little chocolate spread.

Makes 750 g (1½ lb) loaf
Time 2 hours 50 minutes–4 hours, *depending on machine*

250 ml (8 fl oz) water

2 tablespoons sunflower oil

1 teaspoon salt

½ teaspoon ground cinnamon

½ teaspoon ground allspice

1 teaspoon dried chilli seeds

400 g (13 oz) strong white flour

40 g (1½ oz) cocoa

3 tablespoons dark muscovado sugar

1¼ teaspoons fast-action dried yeast

100 g (3½ oz) ready-to-eat dried figs, diced

1 Lift the bread pan out of the bread machine and fit the kneader blade. Add the water, oil, salt, spices and chilli seeds. Spoon in the flour and cocoa, make a slight dip in the centre and add the sugar and yeast.

2 Insert the pan into the bread machine. Shut the lid and set to a 750 g (1½ lb) loaf on a basic white setting with preferred crust setting. Press start.

3 When the raisin beep sounds, gradually add the figs.

4 At the end of the programme, lift the pan out of the machine using oven gloves. Loosen the bread with a plastic spatula, turn it out on to a wire rack and leave to cool.

Tip You could use 1 teaspoon of fresh chopped red chilli instead of the dried seeds, but choose a large, mild chilli rather than the tiny, red-hot Thai chillies.

Sweet breads

Cheat's stollen

Packed with all the seasonal flavour of a true German Christmas stollen, this machine-made version is speckled with diced marzipan rather than being wrapped around a ribbon of marzipan.

Makes 750 g (1½ lb) loaf
Time 2 hours 50 minutes–4 hours, *depending on machine*

175 ml (6 fl oz) milk

50 g (2 oz) butter, melted

1 egg, beaten

grated rind of 1 lemon

½ teaspoon salt

½ teaspoon grated nutmeg

4 cardamom pods, seeds crushed and pods discarded

375 g (12 oz) strong white flour

50 g (2 oz) caster sugar

1¼ teaspoons fast-action dried yeast

75 g (3 oz) mixed dried fruit

50 g (2 oz) glacé cherries, roughly chopped

75 g (3 oz) yellow marzipan, diced

To finish

1 tablespoon butter

2 tablespoons icing sugar, sifted

1 Lift the bread pan out of the bread machine and fit the kneader blade. Add the milk, butter and beaten egg, then the lemon rind, salt and spices. Spoon the flour over the top and add the sugar. Make a slight dip in the centre and sprinkle in the yeast.

2 Insert the pan into the bread machine. Shut the lid and set to a 750 g (1½ lb) loaf on a sweet setting with a medium crust. Press start.

3 When the raisin beep sounds, gradually add the fruit and marzipan.

4 At the end of the programme, lift the pan out of the machine using oven gloves. Loosen the bread with a plastic spatula, turn it out on to a wire rack. Rub the top with the butter and dust heavily with sifted icing sugar. Leave to cool.

Tip Add the dried fruits and marzipan in small batches so that the kneader blade does not get jammed.

Note Do not use the delay timer programme because this bread contains milk and eggs.

Chunky chocolate and vanilla bread

During mixing you will find that some of the chocolate melts and some of the chunks remain whole. If you are making this for children you might prefer to add milk chocolate instead.

Makes 750 g (1½ lb) loaf
Time 2 hours 50 minutes–
4 hours, *depending on machine*

1 egg, beaten

1 egg yolk

50 g (2 oz) butter, melted

175 ml (6 fl oz) milk

½ teaspoon salt

2 teaspoons vanilla extract

400 g (13 oz) strong white flour

50 g (2 oz) caster sugar

1¼ teaspoons fast-action dried yeast

125 g (4 oz) plain dark chocolate, diced

1 Lift the bread pan out of the bread machine and fit the kneader blade. Add the whole egg, egg yolk, butter, milk, salt and vanilla extract. Spoon in the flour, make a slight dip in the centre and add the sugar and yeast.

2 Insert the pan into the bread machine. Shut the lid and set to a 750 g (1½ lb) loaf on a sweet setting with a light crust. Press start.

3 When the raisin beep sounds, gradually add the chocolate.

4 At the end of the programme, lift the pan out of the machine using oven gloves. Loosen the bread with a plastic spatula, turn it out on to a wire rack and leave to cool.

Tip For an extra chocolaty finish, dust the top of the bread with a little sifted cocoa.

Note Do not use the delay timer programme with this recipe.

Dried fruit fiesta

This light, sweet, fresh-tasting loaf, subtly flavoured with a just a hint of lemon and orange rind, is generously speckled with energy- and mineral-boosting diced dried fruits.

Makes 750 g (1½ lb) loaf
Time 2 hours 50 minutes–4 hours, *depending on machine*

200 ml (7 fl oz) water

1 egg, beaten

grated rind of 1 lemon

grated rind of 1 orange

2 tablespoons butter, at room temperature

½ teaspoon salt

375 g (12 oz) strong white flour

3 tablespoons caster sugar

1 teaspoon fast-action dried yeast

175 g (6 oz) dried fruit boost or diced mixed dried fruits

sifted icing sugar, to finish

1 Lift the bread pan out of the bread machine and fit the kneader blade. Add the water, egg, lemon and orange rind, butter and salt. Spoon in the flour, make a slight dip in the centre and add the sugar and yeast.

2 Insert the pan into the bread machine. Shut the lid and set to a 750 g (1½ lb) loaf on a sweet setting with a light crust. Press start.

3 When the raisin beep sounds, gradually add the dried fruit.

4 At the end of the programme, lift the pan out of the machine using oven gloves. Loosen the bread with a plastic spatula, turn it out on to a wire rack. Dust the top with a little sifted icing sugar and leave to cool.

Tip Most supermarkets now stock ready-diced mixed dried fruits as healthy snack foods, but you may prefer to make up your own mix with dried fruits that you already have in the larder, or you could use trail mix, a combination of banana chips, dried fruit and coconut shavings.

Note Do not use the delay timer programme with this recipe.

Chocolate and pecan panettone

A rich, dark, Italian-style bread made with a mix of grated dark chocolate and cocoa, generously enriched with beaten eggs, butter and extra sugar.

Makes 750 g (1½ lb) loaf
Time 2 hours 50 minutes–4 hours

1 egg, beaten

1 egg yolk

50 g (2 oz) butter, melted

175 ml (6 fl oz) milk

½ teaspoon salt

50 g (2 oz) plain dark chocolate, grated

25 g (1 oz) cocoa

375 g (12 oz) white bread flour

50 g (2 oz) caster sugar

1¼ teaspoons fast-action dried yeast

50 g (2 oz) pecan nuts, halved

1 Lift the bread pan out of the bread machine and fit the kneader blade. Add the whole egg, egg yolk, butter, milk and salt. Spoon in the grated chocolate and cocoa. Spoon the flour on top, make a slight dip in the centre and add the sugar and yeast.

2 Insert the pan into the bread machine. Shut the lid and set to 750 g (1½ lb) loaf on a sweet setting with a light crust. Press start.

3 When the raisin beep sounds, gradually add the pecan nuts.

4 At the end of the programme, lift the pan out of the machine using oven gloves. Loosen the bread with a plastic spatula, turn it out on to a wire rack and leave to cool.

Tip The richer the bread the slower it is to rise, so extra yeast is required to boost the rise of this dark chocolaty bread. If you do not like nuts simply leave them out or add 75 g (3 oz) chopped prunes or figs instead.

Note Do not use the delay timer programme with this recipe.

Spiced fruit bread

This fruit bread has all the flavour of a hot cross bun but baked as a loaf. Brush the top with a hot milk and sugar glaze at the end for the characteristic shiny finish.

Makes 750 g (1½ lb) loaf
Time 2 hours 50 minutes–4 hours, *depending on machine*

200 ml (7 fl oz) water

1 tablespoon milk powder

1 egg, beaten

2 tablespoons butter, at room temperature

½ teaspoon salt

2 teaspoons ground mixed spice

425 g (14 oz) strong white flour

3 tablespoons caster sugar

1 teaspoon fast-action dried yeast

125 g (4 oz) raisins or sultanas

25 g (1 oz) chopped candied peel

To glaze

2 tablespoons milk

1 tablespoon caster sugar

1 Lift the bread pan out of the bread machine and fit the kneader blade. Add the water, milk powder, egg, butter, salt and spice. Spoon in the flour, make a slight dip in the centre and add the sugar and yeast.

2 Insert the pan into the bread machine. Shut the lid and set to a 750 g (1½ lb) loaf on a sweet setting with a light crust. Press start.

3 When the raisin beep sounds, gradually add the dried fruit and peel.

4 At the end of the programme, lift the pan out of the machine using oven gloves. Loosen the bread with a plastic spatula, turn it out on to a wire rack.

5 Make the glaze by heating the milk and sugar together in a small saucepan. Bring to the boil, brush over the hot loaf and leave to cool.

Tip If you prefer use 150 g (5 oz) luxury mixed fruit instead of the raisins or sultanas and candied peel.

Note Do not use the delay timer programme with this recipe.

Spiced muesli bread

This light-textured, well-risen loaf is speckled with breakfast cereal and has just a hint of sweetness. It's delicious topped with butter and jam or toasted and simply buttered.

Makes 750 g (1½ lb) loaf
Time 2 hours 50 minutes–4 hours, *depending on machine*

250 ml (8 fl oz) water

2 tablespoons milk powder

2 tablespoons butter, at room temperature

½ teaspoon salt

2 teaspoons ground cinnamon

175 g (6 oz) luxury fruit and nut muesli, plus extra to finish

375 g (12 oz) strong white flour

2 tablespoons set honey

1 teaspoon fast-action dried yeast

egg yolk and water, to glaze (see page 15)

1 Lift the bread pan out of the bread machine and fit the kneader blade. Add the water, milk powder, butter, salt and cinnamon. Spoon the muesli and flour over the top, make a slight dip in the centre and add the honey and yeast.

2 Insert the pan into the bread machine. Shut the lid and set to a 750 g (1½ lb) loaf on a basic white bread setting with the preferred crust setting. Press start.

3 Just before baking begins, brush the top with egg glaze and sprinkle with extra muesli. Close the lid gently.

4 At the end of the programme, lift the pan out of the machine using oven gloves. Loosen the side of the bread with a plastic spatula, turn it out on to a wire rack and leave to cool.

Tip If you choose a luxury muesli you will be guaranteed 50 per cent nuts and fruit, which may include a range of ingredients, such as coconut shreds, halved almonds or hazelnuts, diced papaya or pineapple, raisins or sultanas.

Gingered papaya and pineapple bread

This nicely domed loaf makes a great mid-afternoon treat served warm with butter and apricot jam, or it can be toasted for breakfast. Use any leftovers to make French toast and serve with yogurt and sliced peaches.

Makes 750 g (1½ lb) loaf
Time 2 hours 50 minutes–4 hours, *depending on machine*

250 ml (8 fl oz) ginger beer

2 tablespoons sunflower oil

2 tablespoons ready-chopped glacé ginger

½ teaspoon salt

425 g (14 oz) strong white flour

3 tablespoons caster sugar

1 teaspoon fast-action dried yeast

125 g (4 oz) pack ready-diced dried mixed papaya and pineapple

1 Lift the bread pan out of the bread machine and fit the kneader blade. Add the ginger beer, oil, chopped ginger and salt. Spoon in the flour, make a slight dip in the centre and add the sugar and yeast.

2 Insert the pan into the bread machine. Shut the lid and set to a 750 g (1½ lb) loaf on a sweet setting with a medium crust. Press start.

3 When the raisin beep sounds, gradually add the fruit mix.

4 At the end of the programme, lift the pan out of the machine using oven gloves. Loosen the bread with a plastic spatula, turn it out on to a wire rack and leave to cool.

Tip If you like, roughly crush some sugar lumps and sprinkle over the loaf just before baking.

Coconut and cranberry bread

A golden crusted bread dotted with jewel-like ruby-red cranberries and speckled with white coconut. Serve warm or toasted with strawberry jam.

Makes 750 g (1½ lb) loaf
Time 2 hours 50 minutes–4 hours, *depending on machine*

250 ml (8 fl oz) water

2 tablespoons milk powder

2 tablespoons butter, at room temperature

½ teaspoon salt

40 g (1½ oz) desiccated coconut

425 g (14 oz) strong white flour

3 tablespoons caster sugar

1 teaspoon fast-action dried yeast

100 g (3½ oz) dried cranberries

1 Lift the bread pan out of the bread machine and fit the kneader blade. Add the water, milk powder, butter, salt and coconut. Spoon in the flour, make a slight dip in the centre and add the sugar and yeast.

2 Insert the pan into the bread machine. Shut the lid and set to a 750 g (1½ lb) loaf on a sweet setting with a pale crust. Press start.

3 When the raisin beep sounds, gradually add the cranberries.

4 At the end of the programme, lift the pan out of the machine using oven gloves. Loosen the bread with a plastic spatula, turn it out on to a wire rack and leave to cool.

Tip You could use a mix of dried berries, including blueberries, cherries and cranberries, or try this recipe with 100 g (3½ oz) diced ready-to-eat apricots.

Soured cream and summer berry bread

Although dried fruits have been used instead of fresh, they plump up beautifully as the bread rises and combine with the creaminess of the crème fraîche to make a bread with a wonderfully soft crust.

Makes 750 g (1½ lb) loaf
Time 2 hours 50 minutes–4 hours

150 ml (¼ pint) water

150 g (5 oz) full-fat crème fraîche

½ teaspoon salt

grated rind of 1 lemon

425 g (14 oz) strong white flour

3 tablespoons caster sugar

1 teaspoon fast-action dried yeast

100 g (3½ oz) mixed dried cherries, blueberries and cranberries

1 Lift the bread pan out of the bread machine and fit the kneader blade. Add the water, crème fraîche, salt and lemon rind. Spoon in the flour, make a slight dip and add the sugar and yeast.

2 Insert the pan into the bread machine. Shut the lid and set to a 750 g (1½ lb) loaf on sweet setting with a medium crust. Press start.

3 When the raisin beep sounds, gradually add the fruit mix.

4 At the end of the programme, remove the pan from the machine using oven gloves. Loosen the bread with a plastic spatula, turn it out on to a wire rack and leave to cool.

Tip Don't be tempted to add fresh berries because they will be crushed by the kneader blade and make the bread dough sloppy.

Note Do not use the delay timer programme with this recipe.

Poppy seed and lemon bread

Speckled with tiny black poppy seeds, this tangy lemon bread is delicious served warm, simply buttered and with no added adornment.

Makes 750 g (1½ lb) loaf
Time 2 hours 50 minutes–
4 hours, *depending on machine*

150 ml (¼ pint) water

1 tablespoon milk powder

2 tablespoons butter, at room temperature

½ teaspoon salt

grated rind and juice of 1 lemon

3 tablespoons poppy seeds

425 g (14 oz) strong white flour

3 tablespoons caster sugar

1 teaspoon fast-action dried yeast

1 Lift the bread pan out of the bread machine and fit the kneader blade. Add the water, milk powder, butter and salt. Add the lemon rind and juice and poppy seeds. Spoon in the flour, make a slight dip in the centre and add the sugar and yeast.

2 Insert the pan into the bread machine. Shut the lid and set to a 750 g (1½ lb) loaf on a sweet setting with a medium crust. Press start.

3 At the end of the programme, lift the pan out of the machine using oven gloves. Loosen the bread with a plastic spatula, turn it out on to a wire rack and leave to cool.

Tip As a variation, the grated rind and juice of a small orange can be used instead of the lemon rind and juice.

Shaped breads

Red onion and sun-dried tomato schiacciata

This impressive bread is made with two layers of foccacia bread sandwiched with garlicky fried and caramelized red onion, thickly sliced sun-dried tomatoes, spoonfuls of pesto and fresh basil leaves.

Makes 1 round bread
Time 1½ hours in the bread machine, plus 20–30 minutes rising and 25 minutes baking

275 ml (9 fl oz) water

3 tablespoons olive oil

1 teaspoon salt

475 g (15 oz) strong plain white flour

2 teaspoons caster sugar

1½ teaspoons fast-action dried yeast

To finish

4 tablespoons olive oil

1 large red onion, thinly sliced

2 garlic cloves, finely chopped

1 teaspoon caster sugar

3 teaspoons black olive or sun-dried tomato pesto

50 g (2 oz) sun-dried tomatoes, drained and sliced

small bunch of fresh basil

a few coarse salt flakes

1 Lift the bread pan out of the bread machine and fit the kneader blade. Add the water, oil and salt. Spoon in the flour, make a slight dip in the centre and add the sugar and yeast.

2 Insert the pan into the bread machine. Shut the lid and set to dough. Press start.

3 Just before the end of the programme, prepare the filling for the bread by heating 1 tablespoon oil in a frying pan. Add the onion and garlic and fry gently for 5 minutes until softened. Scoop out one-quarter and reserve for the topping. Add the sugar to the remaining onions and cook for a few minutes more until caramelized.

4 At the end of the dough programme, lift the pan out of the bread machine and scoop out the dough. Knead well on a lightly floured surface and cut in half.

5 Roll one-half out to a rough circle about 23 cm (9 inches) in diameter. Put it on an oiled baking sheet. Press holes over the bread with the end of the handle of a wooden spoon then spread with the pesto. Top with the caramelized onions and three-quarters of the sun-dried tomatoes. Add half the basil leaves and drizzle with 1 tablespoon oil.

6 Roll out the remaining dough to a circle and cover the first circle. Mark with the end of a wooden spoon handle and sprinkle with the remaining onions, tomatoes and basil leaves. Sprinkle with a little salt and drizzle with 1 more tablespoon of oil. Cover loosely with oiled clingfilm and leave to rise in a warm place for 30 minutes.

7 Remove the clingfilm and bake the bread in a preheated oven, 200°C (400°F), Gas Mark 6, for 25 minutes until golden brown and the centre is cooked through. Transfer to a chopping board, drizzle with the remaining oil and serve warm, cut into wedges, with cold meats and salad or bowls of soup.

Garlicky olive and rosemary foccacia

There's no fiddly garlic peeling to do with this recipe: just buy green olives stuffed with garlic and then roughly chop them before use. Serve the bread while it's still warm at summer barbecues.

Makes 2 loaves
Time 1½ hours in the bread machine, plus 20–30 minutes rising and 15 minutes cooking

275 ml (9 fl oz) water

3 tablespoons olive oil

1 teaspoon salt

475 g (15 oz) strong white flour

1 teaspoon caster sugar

1¼ teaspoons fast-action dried yeast

To finish

50 g (2 oz) pitted black olives

75 g (3 oz) pitted green olives stuffed with garlic

small bunch of fresh rosemary

coarse salt

4 tablespoons olive oil

1 Lift the bread pan out of the bread machine and fit the kneader blade. Add the water, oil and salt. Spoon in the flour, make a slight dip in the centre and add the sugar and yeast.

2 Insert the pan into the bread machine. Shut the lid and set to dough. Press start.

3 At the end of the programme, lift the pan out of the machine, scoop out the dough and knead well on a lightly floured surface.

4 Roughly chop the olives and roughly chop a little of the rosemary to give about 1 tablespoon. Knead these into the bread dough. Cut the dough in half and pat each portion into a rough oval, about 23 x 15 cm (9 x 6 inches), and transfer to a large oiled baking sheet.

5 Press tiny sprigs of rosemary into the dough and sprinkle with a little salt. Cover with oiled clingfilm and leave in a warm place for 20–30 minutes until well risen.

6 Remove the clingfilm and drizzle each bread with 1 tablespoon oil. Bake in a preheated oven, 200°C (400°F), Gas Mark 6, for 15 minutes until golden and the bread sounds hollow when tapped. Drizzle the loaves with the remaining oil and transfer to a wire rack to cool.

Tip If you don't much care for olives, add roughly chopped sun-dried tomatoes instead and top the foccacias with tiny cherry tomatoes and sprigs of rosemary.

Cracked pepper and Parmesan grissini

Serve these crisp Italian breadsticks with pre-dinner drinks or with a selection of mixed hams, salami, olives and tomatoes as part of an antipasto (cold hors d'oeuvres) platter.

Makes 30
Time 1½ hours in the bread machine, plus 20–30 minutes rising and 6 minutes baking

275 ml (9 fl oz) water

3 tablespoons olive oil

1 teaspoon salt

1 teaspoon coloured peppercorns, roughly crushed

75 g (3 oz) fresh Parmesan cheese, finely grated, plus extra to finish

475 g (15 oz) strong white flour

1 teaspoon caster sugar

1¼ teaspoons fast-action dried yeast

To finish

egg yolk and water (see page 15)

coarse sea salt

1 Lift the bread pan out of the bread machine and fit the kneader blade. Add the water, oil, salt, peppercorns and Parmesan. Spoon in the flour, make a slight dip in the centre and add the sugar and yeast.

2 Insert the pan into the bread machine. Shut the lid and set to dough. Press start.

3 At the end of the programme, lift the pan out of the machine, scoop out the dough and knead well on a lightly floured surface.

4 Cut the dough into 30 pieces and shape each piece into a rope about 25 cm (10 inches) long. Transfer them to 2 large oiled baking sheets, leaving a little space between each grissini. Cover with lightly oiled clingfilm and leave in a warm place to rise for 20–30 minutes.

5 Remove the clingfilm and brush the grissini with the egg and water mix. Sprinkle half with a little extra grated Parmesan and the rest with a little coarse salt. Bake in a preheated oven, 220°C (425°F), Gas Mark 7, for about 6 minutes until golden. Transfer to a wire rack and leave to cool.

Tip You could try flavouring the grissini with a few crushed fennel seeds, fresh chopped rosemary or thyme leaves or just salt and cracked peppercorns, although if you are making these for children you might prefer to omit the peppercorns.

Wholewheat rosemary baguettines

These mini brown baguettes are speckled with fresh rosemary and malted wheat grains, and they taste just as good filled with cheese and salad on summer days or hot sausages and fried onions in winter.

Makes 8
Time 1½ hours in the bread machine, plus 20–30 minutes rising and 8 minutes baking

300 ml (½ pint) water

2 tablespoons milk powder

2 tablespoons butter, at room temperature

2 tablespoons chopped fresh rosemary leaves, plus extra to finish

1½ teaspoons salt

500 g (1 lb) strong malthouse flour, plus extra to finish

2 tablespoons dark muscovado sugar

1½ teaspoons fast-action dried yeast

1 Lift the bread pan out of the bread machine and fit the kneader blade. Add the water, milk powder, butter, rosemary and salt. Spoon in the flour, make a slight dip in the centre and add the sugar and yeast.

2 Insert the pan into the bread machine. Shut the lid and set to dough. Press start.

3 At the end of the programme, lift the pan out of the machine, scoop out the dough and knead well on a lightly floured surface.

4 Cut the dough into 8 pieces and shape each piece into an 18 cm (7 inch) long baguette. Transfer them to an oiled baking sheet and slash each one 3 times. Sprinkle with a little extra rosemary, cover with oiled clingfilm and leave to rise in a warm place for 20–30 minutes.

5 Remove the clingfilm and sprinkle the loaves with a little extra flour. Bake in a preheated oven, 220°C (425°F), Gas Mark 7, for about 8 minutes until golden brown and the bread sounds hollow when tapped. Transfer to a wire rack to cool.

Tip You could use fresh thyme or sage leaves, or, if you prefer, leave the bread plain.

Roasted vegetable pizzas

As good, if not better, than restaurant pizzas, this recipe is a great way to get teenagers interested in cooking.

Makes 4 pizzas, each 23 cm (9 inch) across
Time 1½ hours in the bread machine, plus 20–30 minutes rising and 28–30 minutes baking

200 ml (7 fl oz) water

3 tablespoons olive oil

1 teaspoon salt

400 g (13 oz) strong white flour

1 teaspoon caster sugar

1¼ teaspoons fast-action dried yeast

Topping

1 orange pepper, cored, deseeded and quartered

1 yellow or red pepper, cored, deseeded and quartered

1 red onion, cut into thin wedges

2 tablespoons olive oil

500 g (1 lb) cherry tomatoes, halved

2 garlic cloves, finely chopped

salt and pepper

400 g (13 oz) mozzarella, drained and thinly sliced

small bunch of fresh basil

1 Lift the bread pan out of the bread machine and fit the kneader blade. Add the water, oil and salt. Spoon in the flour, make a slight dip in the centre and add the sugar and yeast.

2 Insert the pan into the bread machine. Shut the lid and set to dough. Press start.

3 Meanwhile, make the topping by arranging the peppers, skin side up, in a large roasting tin with the onions. Drizzle over 1 tablespoon oil and roast in a preheated oven, 220°C (425°F), Gas Mark 7, for 10 minutes. Add the tomatoes, garlic and a little salt and pepper, then drizzle with the remaining oil. Roast for a further 10 minutes until the tomatoes are softened and the skins of the peppers are blackened.

4 Leave to cool, then peel off the pepper skins and slice the flesh into strips.

5 At the end of the programme, lift the pan out of the machine, scoop out the dough and knead well on a lightly floured surface.

6 Cut the dough into 4 pieces, roll out each piece thinly to a rough shaped circle about 23 cm (9 inches) in diameter and transfer to 2 large, lightly oiled baking sheets. Spoon the tomatoes, onion and peppers on top then tuck the sliced mozzarella between the vegetables. Sprinkle with a little extra pepper and some basil leaves. Bake in a preheated oven, 220°C (425°F), Gas Mark 7, for 8–10 minutes until pizza edges are browned. Serve immediately.

Tip Depending on the size of your baking sheets you may find it easier to make oval pizzas so that they fit more easily side by side.

Picos

These dainty Spanish-style knots are sprinkled with sesame seeds, but coarse sea salt, roughly chopped herbs or a few fennel seeds could be used instead.

Makes 16
Time 1½ hours in the bread machine, plus 20–30 minutes rising and 8–10 minutes cooking

275 ml (9 fl oz) water

2 tablespoons olive oil

1 teaspoon salt

475 g (15 oz) strong white flour

2 teaspoons caster sugar

1¼ teaspoons fast-action dried yeast

To finish

egg yolk and water (see page 15)

3 tablespoons sesame seeds

1 Lift the bread pan out of the bread machine and fit the kneader blade. Add the water, oil and salt. Spoon in the flour, make a slight dip in the centre and add the sugar and yeast.

2 Insert the pan into the bread machine. Shut the lid and set to dough. Press start.

3 At the end of the programme, lift the pan out of the machine, scoop out the dough and knead well on a lightly floured surface.

4 Cut the dough into 16 pieces and shape each piece into a thin rope about 30 cm (12 inches) long. Knot loosely and put on a large, lightly oiled baking sheet. Cover loosely with oiled clingfilm and leave in a warm place for 20–30 minutes until well risen.

5 Remove the clingfilm. Brush the knots with egg glaze, sprinkle with the sesame seeds and bake in a preheated oven, 200°C (400°F), Gas Mark 6, for 8–10 minutes until golden and the bread sounds hollow when tapped. Transfer to a wire rack to cool.

Devonshire splits

A wonderfully indulgent way to eat freshly made bread rolls. Serve on the day they are made, split and lavishly filled with strawberry jam and clotted cream ... worth breaking the diet for!

Makes 12
Time 1½ hours in the bread machine, plus 20–30 minute rising and 10 minutes baking

300 ml (½ pint) cold water

2 tablespoons milk powder

2 tablespoons butter, at room temperature

½ teaspoon salt

500 g (1 lb) strong white flour

2 teaspoons caster sugar

1¼ teaspoons fast-action dried yeast

To finish

egg yolk and water (see page 15)

250 g (8 oz) strawberry jam

250 g (8 oz) clotted cream

sifted icing sugar

1 Lift the bread pan out of the bread machine and fit the kneader blade. Add the water, milk powder, butter and salt. Spoon the flour over the top then make a slight dip in the centre and add the sugar and yeast.

2 Insert the pan into the bread machine. Shut the lid and set to dough. Press start.

3 At the end of the programme, lift the pan out of the machine, scoop out the dough and knead well on a lightly floured surface.

4 Cut the dough into 12 pieces and shape each piece into a ball. Put them on large, lightly oiled baking sheets, leaving a little space around each one. Cover lightly with oiled clingfilm and leave to rise in a warm place for 20–30 minutes.

5 Remove the clingfilm and brush the rolls with the egg glaze. Bake in a preheated oven, 200°C (400°F), Gas Mark 6, for 10 minutes until golden and the bases sound hollow when tapped with the fingertips. Transfer to a wire rack and leave to cool.

6 When ready to serve, cut a diagonal slice down through the rolls almost but not quite through the base. Spoon the jam into the slit then add spoonfuls of clotted cream. Transfer to serving plates and dust with sifted icing sugar.

Tip You may prefer to fill just 6 rolls and freeze the unfilled ones for another time.

Cheese and chutney picnic rolls

Rather than making sandwiches for a picnic, these tasty little rolls have the filling already added before baking. Serve them with cherry tomatoes and cucumber sticks.

Makes 16
Time 1½ hours in the bread machine, plus 20–30 minutes rising and 10 minutes baking

275 ml (9 fl oz) water

2 tablespoons sunflower oil

1 teaspoon salt

125 g (4 oz) extra mature Cheddar cheese, grated, plus extra to finish

200 g (7 oz) strong wholemeal flour

275 g (9 oz) strong white flour

1 teaspoon caster sugar

1¼ teaspoons fast-action dried yeast

To finish

125 g (4 oz) spiced tomato chutney

egg yolk and water (see page 15)

1 Lift the bread pan out of the bread machine and fit the kneader blade. Add the water, oil, salt and cheese. Spoon in the flours, make a slight dip in the centre and add the sugar and yeast.

2 Insert the pan into the bread machine. Shut the lid and set to dough. Press start.

3 At the end of the programme, lift the pan out of the machine, scoop out the dough and knead well on a lightly floured surface.

4 Cut it into 16 pieces and flatten each piece with your hand. Add a teaspoon of chutney to the centre and pinch the edges of the dough together to enclose the chutney. Turn over the rolls and transfer them to a large, greased baking sheet. Cover with lightly oiled clingfilm and leave in a warm place for about 20–30 minutes until well risen.

5 Remove the clingfilm and brush the rolls with the egg glaze. Sprinkle with a little extra cheese and bake in a preheated oven, 200°C (400°F), Gas Mark 6, for about 10 minutes until golden and the rolls sound hollow when tapped. Transfer them to a wire rack and leave to cool.

Iced buns

These little breads are baked in individual tins then drizzled with orange-flavoured glacé icing and sprinkled with hundreds and thousands. Perfect sliced and served for a dollies' or teddy bears' tea party.

Makes 6

Time 1½ hours in the bread machine, plus 20–30 minutes rising and 12–15 minutes baking

2 eggs, beaten

3 tablespoons milk

2 tablespoons butter, at room temperature

½ teaspoon salt

grated rind of ½ orange

250 g (8 oz) strong white flour

2 tablespoons caster sugar

¾ teaspoon fast-action dried yeast

To finish

100 g (3½ oz) icing sugar, sifted

3–4 teaspoons fresh orange juice

a few sugar sprinkles, such as hundreds and thousands or sugar flowers

1 Lift the bread pan out of the bread machine and fit the kneader blade. Add the eggs, milk, butter, salt and orange rind. Spoon in the flour, make a slight dip in the centre and add the sugar and yeast.

2 Insert the pan into the bread machine. Shut the lid and set to dough. Press start.

3 At the end of the programme, lift the pan out of the bread machine and scoop out the dough. Knead well on a lightly floured surface.

4 Cut the dough into 6 pieces, knead each piece and press into the base of 6 individual buttered tins, each 10 x 5.5 x 3.5 cm (4 x 2¼ x 1½ inches). Cover loosely with oiled clingfilm and leave to rise in a warm place for 20–30 minutes until the dough is just above the tops of the tins.

5 Remove the clingfilm and bake the buns in a preheated oven, 200°C (400°F), Gas Mark 6, for about 10 minutes until golden brown and the bread sounds hollow when tapped. Loosen the bread, tip it out on to a wire rack and remove the tins. Leave to cool.

6 Put the icing sugar in a bowl and gradually stir in the orange juice until smooth and thick. Spoon over the tops of the buns and sprinkle with sugar decorations. Leave for 15 minutes for the icing to harden.

Tip If you don't have any little tins, cut the dough into 9–10 pieces, shape into small oval rolls and leave to rise on a baking sheet. Bake for 10 minutes.

Note Do not use the delay timer programme because this recipe contains raw eggs and fresh milk.

Rabbits

These stylized rabbits are made by twisting a rope of dough and adding a little iced tail. They are fun to make for children's parties, to celebrate Easter or to make with your children to while away a wet afternoon.

Makes 8
Time 1½ hours in the bread machine, plus 20–30 minutes rising and 10–12 minutes baking

1 egg, beaten

150 ml (¼ pint) milk

2 tablespoons butter, at room temperature

½ teaspoon salt

375 g (12 oz) strong white flour

2 tablespoons caster sugar

1 teaspoon fast-action dried yeast

To finish

egg yolk and water (see page 15)

50 g (2 oz) icing sugar, sifted

1 Lift the bread pan out of the bread machine and fit the kneader blade. Add the egg, milk, butter and salt. Spoon in the flour, make a slight dip in the centre and add the sugar and yeast.

2 Insert the pan into the bread machine. Shut the lid and set to dough. Press start.

3 At the end of the programme, lift the pan out of the bread machine and scoop out the dough. Knead well on a lightly floured surface.

4 Cut the dough into 9 pieces and shape 8 of these into ropes about 30 cm (12 inches) long that are fatter in the centre and tapering at the ends. Fold each in half to make a loop then twist once to make a body and again to make a head. Transfer to a greased baking sheet and separate the ends to make the ears.

5 Shape the remaining piece of dough into 8 balls and press on the rabbits for tails. Cover loosely with oiled clingfilm and leave to rise in a warm place for 20–30 minutes.

6 Remove the clingfilm and brush the buns with the egg glaze. Bake in a preheated oven, 200°C (400°F), Gas Mark 6, for 10–12 minutes until golden and the bread sounds hollow when tapped. Transfer to a wire rack to cool.

7 Mix the icing sugar with 1½ teaspoons water to make a smooth, thick icing, spoon over the rabbit tails and leave to harden.

Tip The iced tails can also be dipped into tiny sugar sprinkles or hundreds and thousands to make them more colourful.

Note Do not use the delay timer programme with this recipe.

Chocolate and prune brioches

The richest of all the French breads, this buttery bread is much softer to handle so knead on a well-floured surface and scoop the divided dough into the tins using a spoon.

Makes 12

Time 1½ hours in the bread machine, plus 20–30 minutes rising and 8–10 minutes baking

3 eggs, beaten

75 g (3 oz) butter, melted

½ teaspoon salt

1 teaspoon vanilla extract

250 g (8 oz) strong white flour

2 tablespoons caster sugar

1 teaspoon fast-action dried yeast

100 g (3½ oz) plain dark chocolate, diced

100 g (3½ oz) ready-to-eat stoned prunes, diced

sifted icing sugar, to dust

1 Lift the bread pan out of the bread machine and fit the kneader blade. Add the eggs, butter, salt and vanilla extract. Spoon in the flour, make a slight dip in the centre and add the sugar and yeast.

2 Insert the pan into the bread machine. Shut the lid and set to dough. Press start. Check after a few minutes and scrape down the mixture in the corners if necessary.

3 At the end of the programme, lift the pan out of the machine, scoop out the dough and knead well on a generously floured surface.

4 Knead in the chocolate and prunes, then cut the dough into 12 pieces. Scoop each piece into a buttered fluted 8 cm (3½ inch) brioche tin or use plain individual steamed pudding tins.

5 Put the tins on a baking sheet and cover with a large piece of lightly oiled clingfilm. Leave in a warm place for 20–30 minutes until well risen.

6 Remove the clingfilm and bake the brioches in a preheated oven, 200°C (400°F), Gas Mark 6, for 8–10 minutes until golden and tops sound hollow when tapped.

7 Holding each tin with a cloth, loosen the edges of the brioche with a small knife and turn out on to a wire rack. Dust lightly with icing sugar. Serve warm.

Tip For a more intense vanilla flavour, add vanilla-soaked prunes, available in packs from larger supermarkets, or for chocolate fanatics, omit the prunes altogether and add an extra 50 g (2 oz) of chocolate.

Note Do not use the delay timer programme with this recipe.

Cherry and frangipane twist

This impressive-looking bread is easy to make, although you may find it helpful for a volunteer to hold one end of the rolled dough as you twist it.

Makes 1 large loaf
Time 1½ hours in the bread machine, plus 30–40 minutes rising and 25 minutes baking

250 ml (8 fl oz) water

2 tablespoons milk powder

2 tablespoons butter, at room temperature

1 egg, beaten

½ teaspoon salt

500 g (1 lb) strong white flour

1 tablespoon caster sugar

1¼ teaspoons fast-action dried yeast

Filling

100 g (3½ oz) butter, at room temperature

100 g (3½ oz) caster sugar

1 egg, beaten

100 g (3½ oz) ground almonds

½ teaspoon almond essence

425 g (14 oz) can black cherries, drained

To finish

3 tablespoons milk

3 tablespoons flaked almonds

3 tablespoons icing sugar, sifted

1 Lift the bread pan out of the bread machine and fit the kneader blade. Add the water, milk powder, butter, egg and salt. Spoon in the flour, make a slight dip in the centre and add the sugar and yeast.

2 Insert the pan into the bread machine. Shut the lid and set to dough. Press start.

3 Meanwhile, make the frangipane filling by creaming together the butter and sugar. Add the egg, almonds and almond essence and mix together.

4 At the end of the programme, lift the pan out of the machine, scoop out the dough and knead well on a lightly floured surface. Roll out to a 37 x 30 cm (15 x 12 inch) rectangle.

5 Spread the frangipane over the dough to about 2 cm (¾ inches) in from the edge. Sprinkle the drained cherries over the top, then roll up the dough, starting from one of the longer edges. Twist the rolled-up dough to give a corkscrew effect then carefully transfer it to a greased baking tray. Cover with oiled clingfilm and leave in a warm place for about 30–40 minutes until well risen.

6 Remove the clingfilm and brush the twist with milk. Sprinkle with the flaked almonds and bake in a preheated oven, 200°C (400°F), Gas Mark 6, for about 25 minutes until golden and the bread sounds hollow when tapped. Transfer to a wire rack and dust with icing sugar. Serve warm or cold.

Tip Check the bread after 15 minutes and cover it with foil if the almonds are browning too quickly.

Note Do not use the delay timer programme with this recipe.

Dunking chocolate and orange doughnuts

Wonderfully indulgent, warm orange-flavoured doughnuts, crisp on the outside and light and fluffy on the inside. Serve broken and dunked into a warm chocolate fondue-like sauce.

Makes 12
Time 1½ **hours in the bread machine, plus 20–30 minutes rising and 12 minutes frying**

175 ml (6 fl oz) water

2 tablespoons milk powder

2 eggs, beaten

½ teaspoon salt

grated rind of 1 medium orange

425 g (14 oz) strong white flour

1 tablespoon caster sugar

1¼ teaspoons fast-action dried yeast

Chocolate sauce

100 g (3½ oz) plain dark chocolate, broken into pieces

small knob of butter

2 tablespoons icing sugar

2 tablespoons orange juice

2 tablespoons fresh milk

To finish

oil, for deep frying

50 g (2 oz) caster sugar

1 Lift the bread pan out of the bread machine and fit the kneader blade. Add the water, milk powder, eggs, salt and orange rind. Spoon in the flour, make a slight dip in the centre and add the sugar and yeast.

2 Insert the pan into the bread machine. Shut the lid and set to dough. Press start.

3 At the end of the programme, lift the pan out of the machine, scoop out the dough and knead well on a lightly floured surface. Roll it out to 1 cm (½ inch) thick and stamp out 8 cm (3 inch) rounds with a plain biscuit cutter, rerolling the trimmings until you have 12 circles.

4 Make a hole in the centre of each with a finger, then place them on 2 baking sheets lined with oiled clingfilm. Cover loosely with more oiled clingfilm and leave in a warm place for 20–30 minutes until well risen.

5 Meanwhile, make the sauce by melting the chocolate, butter and sugar in a bowl set over a saucepan of simmering water. Stir in the orange juice and milk.

6 Half-fill a large, deep saucepan with oil and heat to 180°C (350°F) on a sugar thermometer or until a cube of bread sizzles the minute it is added. Carefully add the doughnuts, one at a time, until there are three in the pan. Cook for 1–2 minutes until the underside is golden then turn over and cook the other side.

7 Carefully lift out the doughnuts with a slotted spoon and drain on a plate lined with kitchen paper. Continue cooking the remaining doughnuts in the same way.

8 Transfer the doughnuts to a baking sheet lined with greaseproof paper, sprinkle with the caster sugar and drizzle with a little of the chocolate sauce. Serve the remaining sauce separately so that the doughnuts can be broken and dunked. They are best eaten within an hour of cooking.

Apple and ginger coils

A rich, sweet bread is rolled around a poached apple compote speckled with dried fruits and fiery chopped glacé ginger, then glazed with sugar.

Makes 12
Time 1½ hours in the bread machine, plus 30 minutes rising and 20–25 minutes baking

2 eggs, beaten

175 ml (6 fl oz) milk

2 tablespoons butter, at room temperature

½ teaspoon salt

500 g (1 lb) strong white flour

50 g (2 oz) caster sugar

1¼ teaspoons fast-action dried yeast

Filling

400 g (13 oz) cooking apples, peeled, quartered, cored and diced

1 tablespoon lemon juice

2 tablespoons water

50 g (2 oz) caster sugar

125 g (4 oz) luxury mixed dried fruit

2 tablespoons ready-chopped glacé ginger

Glaze

2 tablespoons caster sugar

4 tablespoons milk

1 Lift the bread pan out of the bread machine and fit the kneader blade. Add the eggs, milk, butter and salt. Spoon in the flour, make a slight dip in the centre and add the sugar and yeast.

2 Insert the pan into the bread machine. Shut the lid and set to dough. Press start.

3 Meanwhile, make the filling. Put the apples into a small saucepan with the lemon juice, water, sugar and dried fruit. Cover and simmer for 5 minutes until the apples are just beginning to soften. Remove the lid and cook for 3–5 minutes more until the liquid has evaporated and the apples are tender and the dried fruits are plumped up. Stir in the ginger and leave to cool.

4 At the end of the programme, lift the pan out of the bread machine, scoop out the dough and knead well on a lightly floured surface. Roll out into a large rectangle, 37 x 30 cm (15 x 12 inches).

5 Spread the apple mixture over the dough to within about 2 cm (¾ inch) of the edges. Roll it up, starting from one of the longer edges.

6 Cut the dough into 12 thick slices and arrange the pieces, cut sides up, in 3 rows of 4 coils in a buttered roasting tin, with a base measurement of 30 x 20 cm (12 x 8 inches). Cover loosely with oiled clingfilm and leave to rise in a warm place for 30 minutes.

7 Remove the clingfilm and bake the bread in a preheated oven, 200°C (400°F), Gas Mark 6, for 20–25 minutes until golden and the central coils sound hollow when tapped. When they are almost ready, make the glaze by heating together the sugar and milk until the sugar has dissolved. Boil for 1 minute, then brush over the hot bread. Leave to cool in the tin.

Note Do not use the delay timer programme because this recipe contains raw eggs and milk.

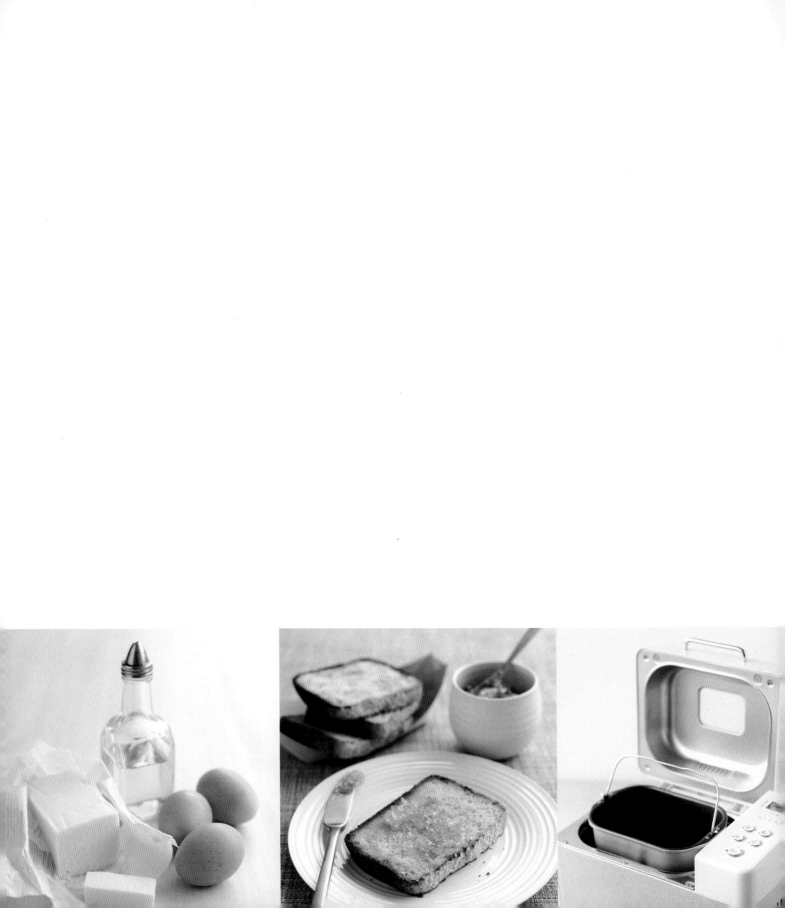

Wheat- and gluten-free breads

Breakfast bread

Wheat-free breads can be very close textured, because they lack the elasticity that gluten gives. To get round this, choose wheat-free flour with added natural gum for a lighter bread with a more open texture.

Makes 750 g (1½ lb) loaf
Time 1 hour–1 hour 10 minutes, *depending on machine*

350 ml (12 fl oz) warm water

4 tablespoons olive oil

2 eggs, beaten

1 teaspoon salt

1 teaspoon vinegar

500 g (1 lb) wheat- and gluten-free white bread flour with natural gum

2 tablespoons sesame seeds, plus extra to finish

2 tablespoons light muscovado sugar

2 teaspoons fast-action dried yeast

small knob of butter, to glaze

1 Lift the bread pan out of the bread machine and fit the kneader blade. Add the warm water, oil, eggs, salt and vinegar. Spoon the flour and sesame seeds over the top. Make a slight dip in the centre and add the sugar and yeast.

2 Insert the pan into the bread machine. Shut the lid and set to a 750 g (1½ lb) loaf on fastbake or rapid setting. Press start.

3 At the end of the programme, lift the pan out of the machine using oven gloves. Loosen the sides of the bread with a plastic spatula and turn it out on to a wire rack. Brush the top with the butter and sprinkle with sesame seeds. Brown the top under the grill.

Tip If you do not have a fastbake or rapid facility on your bread machine then cook on the basic white programme, adding cold water instead of warm and keeping the yeast at 2 teaspoons.

Note Do not use the delay timer programme because this recipe contains eggs.

Banana and sultana bread

The riper the banana the stronger the taste, so this easy recipe is a good way to use up any brown-speckled bananas that are hanging around in your fruit bowl.

Makes 750 g (1½ lb) loaf
Time 1 hour–1 hour 10 minutes, *depending on machine*

1 ripe banana, 200 g (7 oz) with skin on, peeled

2 teaspoons lemon juice

350 ml (12 fl oz) warm water

2 eggs, beaten

4 tablespoons sunflower oil

½ teaspoon salt

500 g (1 lb) wheat- and gluten-free bread flour with added natural gum

2 tablespoons light muscovado sugar

2 teaspoons fast-action dried yeast

75 g (3 oz) sultanas

melted butter, to finish

1 Slice the banana on to a plate, then mash with the lemon juice.

2 Lift the bread pan out of the bread machine and fit the kneader blade. Add the banana, warm water, eggs, oil and salt. Spoon in the flour, make a slight dip in the centre and add the sugar and yeast. Sprinkle the sultanas over the top.

3 Insert the pan into the bread machine. Shut the lid and set to a 750 g (1½ lb) loaf on a fastbake or rapid setting. Press start.

4 At the end of the programme, lift the pan out of the machine using oven gloves. Loosen the bread with a plastic spatula and turn it out on to a wire rack. Brush with the butter and brown under the grill if liked. Leave to cool.

Tip Wheat-free and gluten-free breads are best eaten on the day that they are made, or served toasted for breakfast on the following day.

Note Do not use the delay timer programme with this recipe as warm water is added.

Seeded buckwheat bread

Don't be put off by the buckwheat flour: it is not made from a wheat derivative, but is actually related to the rhubarb family and so is low in gluten. It's bitter, earthy flavour mixes well with the seeds in this loaf.

Makes 750 g (1½ lb) loaf
Time 1 hour to 1 hour 10 minutes, *depending on machine*

350 m (12 fl oz) warm water

2 eggs, beaten

4 tablespoons sunflower oil

1 teaspoon white wine vinegar

1 teaspoon salt

3 tablespoons sunflower seeds

3 tablespoons golden linseeds

3 tablespoons pumpkin seeds

100 g (3 ½ oz) buckwheat flour

375 g (12 oz) wheat- and gluten-free bread flour with natural gum

2 tablespoons light muscovado sugar

2 teaspoons fast-action dried yeast

1 Lift the bread pan out of the bread machine and fit the kneader blade. Add the water, eggs, oil, vinegar and salt. Spoon in the seeds, then add the flours. Make a slight dip in the centre and add the sugar and yeast.

2 Insert the pan into the bread machine. Shut the lid and set to a 750 g (1½ lb) loaf on a fastbake or rapid setting. Press start.

3 At the end of the programme, lift the pan out of the machine using oven gloves. Loosen the bread with a plastic spatula, turn it out on to a wire rack and leave to cool.

Tip Because wheat-free loaves stale more quickly than wheat breads, slice and freeze them as soon as they are cold, then defrost as many slices as you need for a sandwich.

Note Buckwheat flour does contain small amounts of gluten so it is unsuitable for those with coeliac disease. Do not use the delay timer with this recipe.

Spiced coriander and lentil bread

Even though you may not be able to eat naan breads with a curry if you're on a gluten-free diet, this tasty Indian spiced bread makes a delicious substitute. Eat it while it's still warm from the bread maker.

Makes 750 g (1½ lb) loaf
Time 1 hour–1 hour 10 minutes, *depending on machine*

200 g (7 oz) can green lentils, drained and rinsed

350 ml (12 fl oz) warm water

2 eggs, beaten

4 tablespoons sunflower oil

1 teaspoon white wine vinegar

1 teaspoon salt

1 teaspoon paprika

½ teaspoon turmeric

2 teaspoons coriander seeds, roughly crushed

2 teaspoons cumin seeds, roughly crushed

15 g (½ oz) fresh coriander, roughly chopped

400 g (13 oz) wheat- and gluten-free bread flour with added natural gum

2 teaspoons caster sugar

2 teaspoons fast-action dried yeast

1 Put the drained lentils on to a plate and mash them roughly with a fork.

2 Lift the bread pan out of the bread machine and fit the kneader blade. Add the lentils, water, eggs, oil and vinegar. Spoon in the salt, ground and roughly crushed spices, then the coriander. Add the flour, make a slight dip in the centre and add the sugar and yeast.

3 Insert the pan into the bread machine. Shut the lid and set to a 750 g (1½ lb) loaf on a fastbake or rapid setting. Press start.

4 At the end of the programme, lift the pan out of the machine using oven gloves. Loosen the bread with a plastic spatula, turn it out on to a wire rack and leave to cool.

Tip If you would rather use dried lentils that you have cooked at home instead of canned, use 125 g (4 oz) cooked drained weight.

Note Do not use the delay timer with this recipe as warm water is added.

Roasted red pepper and chilli corn bread

This American favourite is made with ground corn or masa harina. Look out for it in the supermarket alongside the speciality ingredients from around the world. Serve with chillied beef or bean mixtures.

Makes 750 g (1½ lb) loaf
Time 1 hour–1 hour 10 minutes, *depending on machine*

1 red pepper, cored, deseeded and quartered

1 tablespoon olive oil

350 ml (12 fl oz) fresh milk, warmed

2 eggs, beaten

50 g (2 oz) butter, melted

50 g (2 oz) Parmesan cheese, grated

1 large fresh mild red chilli, deseeded and finely chopped

1 teaspoon salt

1 teaspoon white wine or malt vinegar

125 g (4 oz) fine ground corn (masa harina)

300 g (10 oz) wheat- and gluten-free bread flour with added natural gum

2 teaspoons caster sugar

2 teaspoons fast-action dried yeast

4 spring onions, chopped

melted butter, to glaze

1 Put the pepper quarters, skin side up, on the grill rack, brush with oil and grill for 10 minutes until the skins are blackened. Wrap in foil, leave to cool then peel off the skins and roughly chop the flesh.

2 Lift the bread pan out of the bread machine and fit the kneader blade. Add the warm milk, eggs, melted butter, Parmesan, chilli, salt and vinegar. Spoon in the ground corn and flour, make a slight dip in the centre and add the sugar and yeast. Spoon the chopped peppers and spring onions on top.

3 Insert the pan into the bread machine. Shut the lid and set to a 750 g (1½ lb) loaf on a fastbake or rapid setting. Press start.

4 At the end of the programme, lift the pan out of the machine using oven gloves. Loosen the bread with a plastic spatula then turn it out on to a wire rack. Brush the top with the butter and brown under the grill, if liked. Leave to cool.

Tip You can use 1 teaspoon of ready-chopped red chilli from a jar or 1 teaspoon dried chilli seeds instead of the fresh chilli.

Note Do not use the delay timer programme with this recipe.

Sunflower seed, yogurt and apricot bread

This healthy breakfast bread has your favourite ingredients already mixed in. Serve warm or toasted, or, when stale, dip it in beaten egg and fry in a little butter then top with a little extra yogurt and some blueberries.

Makes 750 g (1½ lb) loaf
Time 1 hour–1 hour
10 minutes, *depending on machine*

2 eggs, beaten

4 tablespoons sunflower oil

150 ml (5 fl oz) Greek yogurt

250 ml (8 fl oz) warm water

1 teaspoon salt

475 g (15 oz) wheat- and gluten-free bread flour with natural gum

2 tablespoons light muscovado sugar

2 teaspoons fast-action dried yeast

50 g (2 oz) sunflower seeds

125 g (4 oz) ready-to-eat dried apricots, diced

sifted icing sugar, to finish

1 Lift the bread pan out of the bread machine and fit the kneader blade. Add the eggs, oil, yogurt, water and salt. Spoon in the flour, make a slight dip in the centre and add the sugar and yeast. Spoon the seeds and diced apricots on top.

2 Insert the pan into the bread machine. Shut the lid and set to a 750 g (1½ lb) loaf on fastbake or rapid setting. Press start.

3 At the end of the programme, lift the pan out of the machine using oven gloves. Loosen the sides of the bread with a plastic spatula, then turn it out on to a grill rack. Dust with icing sugar then grill until browned. Leave to cool.

Tip You may find that wheat-free breads have a paler top than more conventional breads. Brush with melted butter, egg yolk glaze, or top with a little sugar as here, then grill if liked.

Note Do not use the delay timer setting with this recipe.

Teabreads

Marmalade and raisin teabread

This tangy fruit bread keeps for up to a week in a biscuit tin; just slice it as required and serve spread with a little butter.

Makes 750 g (1½ lb) loaf
Time 1 hour 40 minutes–
1 hour 50 minutes,
depending on machine

grated rind and juice of 1 orange

2 tablespoons chunky orange marmalade

200 g (7 oz) raisins

1 egg, beaten

125 g (4 oz) light muscovado sugar

200 g (7 oz) self-raising flour

1 teaspoon baking powder

1 Pour the orange juice into a measuring jug and make it up to 200 ml (7 fl oz) with water. Pour it into a saucepan, add the orange rind and marmalade and heat gently until dissolved. Bring it to the boil, add the raisins then take the pan off the heat and leave to soak for at least 4 hours.

2 Lift the bread pan out of the bread machine and fit the kneader blade. Add the soaked fruit and juice mixture, egg, sugar, flour and baking powder.

3 Insert the pan into the bread machine. Shut the lid and set to cake. Press start. After about 5 minutes, check on the mixture and scrape down the sides of the pan and into the corners with a plastic spatula if necessary.

4 Because programme times vary, test the cake after 1 hour 40 minutes by inserting a skewer into the centre; if it comes out cleanly the bread is ready. Lift the pan out of the machine using oven gloves, loosen the sides of the bread with a plastic spatula and turn it out on to a wire rack. If the skewer is sticky cook it for 10 minutes more or leave in the machine on the keep-warm facility.

Tip Cold tea can be used instead of orange juice and water to soak the fruits. Omit the marmalade and add 1 teaspoon ground cinnamon instead. The teabread recipes tend to be much shallower than yeast breads.

Note Do not use the delay timer programme with this recipe.

Dark gingerbread

Perfect for packed lunches, this dark, sticky gingerbread keeps for up to a week and just gets better with age. Transform it into a pudding with buttery fried bananas and custard.

Makes 750 g (1½ lb) loaf
Time 1 hour 40 minutes–
1 hour 50 minutes,
depending on machine

125 g (4 oz) dark muscovado sugar

175 g (6 oz) golden syrup

100 g (3½ oz) butter

150 ml (¼ pint) milk

2 eggs, beaten

275 g (9 oz) plain flour

½ teaspoon baking powder

1 teaspoon bicarbonate of soda

3 teaspoons ground ginger

1 Put the sugar, syrup and butter into a saucepan and heat together, stirring occasionally, until the butter has melted. Leave to cool for 10 minutes.

2 Lift the bread pan out of the bread machine and fit the kneader blade. Add the milk and eggs, pour in the syrup mixture, then spoon the remaining ingredients on top.

3 Insert the pan into the bread machine. Shut the lid and set to cake. Press start. After about 5 minutes, check on the mixture and scrape down the sides of the pan and into the corners with a plastic spatula if necessary.

4 Because programme times vary, test the cake after 1 hour 40 minutes by inserting a skewer into the centre; if it comes out cleanly the gingerbread is ready. Lift the pan out of the machine using oven gloves, loosen the sides with a plastic spatula and turn it out on to a wire rack to cool. If the skewer is sticky cook for 10 minutes more or leave in the machine on the keep-warm facility.

Tip For an extra strong gingery taste, add 2 tablespoons ready-chopped glacé ginger in addition to the ground ginger.

Note Do not use the delay timer programme with this recipe.

Spiced apple and date bread

This moist, Madeira-style cake keeps well in a cake tin. Slice and add to lunch boxes or serve as a treat with mid-morning coffee.

Makes 750 g (1½ lb) loaf

Time 1 hour 40 minutes–
1 hour 50 minutes,
depending on machine

250 g (8 oz) or 2 Braeburn apples, cored and diced (skins left on)

3 tablespoons water

2 eggs, beaten

125 g (4 oz) butter, melted

150 g (5 oz) caster sugar

250 g (8 oz) self-raising flour

1 teaspoon baking powder

1 teaspoon ground mixed spice

125 g (4 oz) stoned dates, chopped

1 Put the apples in a small saucepan with the water. Cover and simmer for 10 minutes until tender. Leave to cool for 15 minutes.

2 Lift the bread pan out of the bread machine and fit the kneader blade. Add the cooled apples, eggs and melted butter. Spoon in the sugar, flour, baking powder and spice.

3 Insert the pan into the bread machine. Shut the lid and set to cake. Press start. After about 5 minutes, check on the mixture, scrape down the sides of the pan and into the corners with a plastic spatula if necessary and add the dates.

4 Because programme times vary, test the cake after 1 hour 40 minutes by inserting a skewer into the centre; if it comes out cleanly the bread is ready. Lift the pan out of the machine using oven gloves, loosen the sides with a plastic spatula and turn the bread out on to a wire rack to cool. If the skewer is sticky with mixture, set the machine for 10 minutes longer cooking time, or leave the cake still in the machine on the keep-warm facility.

Tip If you don't have any dates, use the same weight of raisins or sultanas.

Note Do not use the delay timer programme with this recipe.

Apricot and pecan soda bread

Made with a mixture of cream of tartar and bicarbonate of soda, this Irish breakfast bread is best served warm, sliced and buttered, or toasted and spread with honey, or topped with clotted cream for afternoon tea.

Makes 750 g (1½ lb) loaf
Time 1 hour 40 to 1 hour 50 minutes, *depending on machine*

200 ml (7 fl oz) milk

1 teaspoon cream of tartar

50 g (2 oz) butter, melted

1 egg, beaten

125 g (4 oz) soft light muscovado sugar

200 g (7 oz) strong wholemeal flour

200 g (7 oz) strong white flour

1 teaspoon bicarbonate of soda

1 teaspoon ground cinnamon

½ teaspoon salt

75 g (3 oz) pecan nuts, roughly chopped

150 g (5 oz) ready-to-eat dried apricots, roughly chopped

1 Lift the bread pan out of the bread machine and fit the kneader blade. Add the milk, cream of tartar, melted butter and beaten egg. Spoon in the sugar, flours, bicarbonate of soda, cinnamon and salt.

2 Insert the pan into the bread machine. Shut the lid and set to cake. Press start. After about 5 minutes check on the mixture, scrape down the sides of the pan with a plastic spatula if necessary and gradually add the nuts and apricots.

3 Because programme times vary, test the bread after 1 hour 40 minutes by inserting a skewer into the centre; if it comes out cleanly the bread is ready. Lift the pan out of the machine using oven gloves, loosen the sides with a plastic spatula and turn it out on to a wire rack. If the skewer is sticky, cook the bread for 10 more minutes or leave it in the machine on the keep-warm facility. Sprinkle with a little extra flour if liked.

Tip For a change, try this recipe with a mixture of walnuts and dates.

Note Do not use the delay timer programme with this recipe.

Tropical banana bread

Quick and easy to put together, this delicious teabread is flavoured with trail mix, a blend of coconut curls, chunky Brazil nuts, a speckling of sultanas and diced papaya and apricots.

Makes 750 g (1½ lb) loaf
Time 1 hour 40 minutes–
1 hour 50 minutes,
depending on machine

2 bananas, about 300 g (10 oz) with skins on, peeled

1 tablespoon lemon juice

2 eggs, beaten

100 g (3 ½ oz) butter, melted

150 g (5 oz) caster sugar

200 g (7 oz) self-raising flour

1 teaspoon baking powder

125 g (4 oz) trail mix

1 Mash the bananas on a plate with the lemon juice.

2 Lift the bread pan out of the bread machine and fit the kneader blade. Add the bananas, eggs and butter. Spoon in the sugar, flour and baking powder.

3 Insert the pan into the bread machine. Shut the lid and set to cake. Press start. After about 5 minutes check on the mixture and scrape down the sides and into the corners with a plastic spatula if necessary. Slice the Brazil nuts in the trail mix and add to the pan with the remaining mix.

4 Because programme times vary, test the cake after 1 hour 40 minutes by inserting a skewer into the centre; if it comes out cleanly the bread is ready. Lift the pan out of the machine using oven gloves, loosen the sides with a plastic spatula and turn the bread out on to a wire rack to cool. If the skewer is sticky, cook the bread for 10 more minutes or leave it in the machine on the keep-warm facility.

Note Do not use the delay timer programme with this recipe.

Sweet potato and chocolate cake

This rich, moist, dark chocolate cake can be served on its own or topped with a vanilla butter frosting and a sprinkling of grated chocolate.

Makes 750 g (1½ lb) loaf
Time 1 hour 40 minutes–
1 hour 50 minutes,
depending on machine

250 g (8 oz) sweet potato, peeled and cut into chunks

2 tablespoons milk

2 eggs, beaten

125 g (4 oz) butter, melted

125 g (4 oz) light muscovado sugar

150 g (5 oz) self-raising flour

25 g (1 oz) cocoa

1 teaspoon ground cinnamon

½ teaspoon bicarbonate of soda

Frosting

50 g (2 oz) butter, at room temperature

100 g (3½ oz) icing sugar, sifted

½ teaspoon vanilla extract

grated chocolate

1 Cook the sweet potato in a saucepan of boiling water for 15 minutes, drain and mash with the milk. Leave to cool.

2 Lift the bread pan out of the bread machine and fit the kneader blade. Add the sweet potato, eggs, melted butter and sugar. Spoon in the flour, cocoa, cinnamon and bicarbonate of soda.

3 Insert the pan into the bread machine. Shut the lid and set to cake. Press start. After about 5 minutes check the mixture and scrape down the sides and into the corners with a plastic spatula if necessary.

4 Because programme times vary, test the cake after 1 hour 40 minutes by inserting a skewer into the centre; if it comes out cleanly the cake is ready. Lift the pan out of the machine using oven gloves, loosen the sides with a plastic spatula and turn it out on to a wire rack to cool. If the skewer is sticky, cook the cake for 10 more minutes or leave it in the machine on the keep-warm facility.

5 Make the frosting by softening the butter in a bowl. Gradually mix in the icing sugar and stir in the vanilla extract. Spread the frosting over the top of the cooled cake and sprinkle with grated chocolate.

Tip Instead of sprinkling the cake with grated chocolate, use a little extra cinnamon or a dusting of cocoa.

Note Do not use the delay timer programme with this recipe.

Index

Acknowledgements

Executive Editor: Nicola Hill
Editor: Charlotte Macey
Executive Art Editor: Sally Bond
Designer: 'ome design
Senior Production Controller: Manjit Sihra
Photographer: Ian Wallace
Food Stylist: Louise Pickford

Special thanks to: Kenwood, Morphy Richards and Panasonic for loaning their bread machines for recipe testing and photography.